THE DIVINE SPIRIT WITH THE HUMAN SPIRIT IN THE EPISTLES

WITNESS LEE

Living Stream Ministry
Anaheim, CA • www.lsm.org

© 2004 Living Stream Ministry

First Edition, November 2004.

ISBN 0-7363-2770-3

Published by

Living Stream Ministry
2431 W. La Palma Ave., Anaheim, CA 92801 U.S.A.
P. O. Box 2121, Anaheim, CA 92814 U.S.A.

Printed in the United States of America

04   05   06   07   08   09   10   /   9   8   7   6   5   4   3   2   1

CONTENTS

PREFACE

This book is composed of messages given by Brother Witness Lee during the Summer Training of 1966 in Los Angeles, California. These messages were not reviewed by the speaker.

CHAPTER ONE

CHRIST IN THE GOSPELS BECOMING THE ALL-INCLUSIVE LIFE-GIVING SPIRIT IN THE ACTS AND THE EPISTLES

Scripture Reading: John 1:1; 4:24; 1:14, 29; 10:10; 1 Cor. 15:45b; 2 Cor. 3:17; 1 Cor. 6:17

In these messages we will cover a great and profound matter, the divine Spirit with the human spirit in the Epistles, from Romans through the book of Revelation. The Epistles come after the four Gospels and the Acts. The Gospels are a full record of the Lord Jesus Christ—who He is, what He did, what He accomplished, and what He attained. After this, the Acts gives us a record of the spread, the propagation, of this Christ, which is the church as the Body of Christ. In the four Gospels we have the Head, and in the Acts we have the Body, the propagation and continuation of the Head. After this, the twenty-two books from Romans to Revelation present a full definition, explanation, and revelation of the wonderful and mysterious economy of God.

CHRIST BEING GOD AS SPIRIT BECOMING MAN AS FLESH

First, we must see not only who Christ is but what He is. The New Testament tells us that Christ is God Himself. John 1:1 says, "In the beginning was the Word, and the Word was with God, and the Word was God." Then 4:24 says, "God is Spirit." Therefore, Christ as God Himself was Spirit. According to who Christ was, we may say that He was God, but according to what Christ was, we must say that He was Spirit. From the beginning He was Spirit, because He was God Himself who is Spirit. Then verse 14 of chapter 1 says that one day the

Word became flesh. Man is flesh just as God is Spirit. By incarnation this very Christ, who was God Himself as Spirit, became flesh as a man. Now, according to who Christ is, we must say that Christ is both God and man, but according to what Christ is, He is both Spirit and flesh. Christ is God, and He is man. Since God is Spirit and man is flesh, Christ is both Spirit and flesh. God became man, and Spirit became flesh.

Christ as God became a man, and Christ as Spirit became flesh because man needed an offering with blood for the purpose of redemption. Man was lost and fallen, so he needed redemption. Only by an offering with blood is it possible for us to be redeemed. Christ as the Spirit had to become flesh in order to be the offering with blood to shed for our sins. John 1:29 says, "Behold, the Lamb of God, who takes away the sin of the world!" If Christ were only Spirit and had not become flesh, He could not have been the Lamb of God. We need to highlight verses 1, 14, and 29 of the first chapter of John in our Bibles. Then when we open to John 1, we will immediately see these three phrases: *the Word was God, the Word became flesh,* and *behold, the Lamb of God, who takes away the sin of the world.* Christ as God Himself became a man, and as Spirit He became flesh, in order to be the Lamb of God to take away all our sins so that we may be redeemed.

CHRIST BECOMING
THE LIFE-GIVING SPIRIT IN RESURRECTION
TO BE LIFE TO US

However, Christ did not come only for redemption. In the same Gospel, verse 10 of chapter 10 is the word of Christ Himself: "I have come that they may have life and may have it abundantly." This was the further purpose of Christ's coming. The first chapter of this book tells us that in the beginning Christ was the very God, but He became flesh to be the Lamb of God to redeem us. However, redemption is not the goal. It is only a procedure for the goal. The goal is that we may have life. For this purpose, Christ took two steps. The first step was to become flesh so that He might be the Lamb of God for redemption, but since He could not be life to us simply as the Lamb of God in the flesh, there was the need of another step. After accomplishing redemption, He took the further step to become the Spirit who gives life (1 Cor. 15:45b; 2 Cor. 3:6, 17).

In eternity past Christ was God, and one day He became flesh, a man, to accomplish redemption. When He went to the cross in His flesh, He was not yet the life-giving Spirit. He was the Lamb of God with flesh to bear the sin of the world and to shed His blood for the cleansing of sin. There at the cross He died as a man in the flesh, accomplishing a full redemption for us sinners in order to solve all the problems between us and God. Because we were fallen, we needed to be redeemed, and because we had become dirty, we needed to be cleansed. This He accomplished by being the Lamb of God who died in the flesh on the cross. This is wonderful, but it is not the goal. It is only the process, the procedure, to reach the goal. The goal is to give us life.

How could Christ give us life and be life to us? It is by means of another step. After being crucified, He was laid in a tomb, and then He resurrected from the dead. In this resurrection He became something else. In His incarnation as God, He became flesh, but now in His resurrection as a man, He became the life-giving Spirit. First Corinthians 15:45b says, "The last Adam became a life-giving Spirit." We should not only underline this passage but also highlight it and circle it. This verse is vital, living, and basic. It is of great importance, but it has been missed by most Christians today. The last Adam, who is Christ in the flesh as a man, became a life-giving Spirit. This is the Spirit who gives life. Thus, we have the two steps which Christ took, incarnation and resurrection.

We must emphasize this for the sake of the young believers, because today in Christianity many important matters have been neglected. There are many teachings telling people what to do and what not to do, but the vital, living items concerning the life of Christ are mostly missed. In the first step of incarnation Christ became flesh to be the redeeming Lamb, and in the second step of resurrection He became the life-giving Spirit. The Lamb is for redemption, and the Spirit is for life.

THE LORD'S GOING FOR HIS COMING BACK
TO THE DISCIPLES AS THE SPIRIT

Chapter 14 is the turning point of the Gospel of John. At the beginning of this chapter the Lord surprised the disciples by telling them that He was about to leave them. The disciples were greatly disappointed at the thought of losing the Lord. Then the Lord told them the truth, the fact, that His going would be not a loss to them but a gain. His going was not His leaving but His coming back; His going was His coming. About sixteen years ago, after we first came to Taiwan, all our children were very young. One day I brought home a big watermelon. Previously, in mainland China we did not have watermelons in the winter time, so a melon at that time seemed like something to treasure. When I placed the watermelon on the dining table, the children were very excited, but when I took it to the kitchen, some of the little ones began to weep. I told them, "Do not be sorrowful. For me to take away the melon is to bring it closer to you." Then I brought the melon to the kitchen where I cut it into slices. When I brought it back, all the children were happy again. I said to them, "Do you see? Taking it to the kitchen was not to take it away; it was to bring it closer to you." Without taking it away and cutting it into slices, it would have been too difficult to receive. We could have only appreciated and admired it. The watermelon needed to be cut in order to be transformed into something that we could receive. This is an illustration of the Lord's word in John 14.

Verses 16 through 20 say, "And I will ask the Father, and He will give you another Comforter, that He may be with you forever, even the Spirit of reality, whom the world cannot receive, because it does not behold Him or know Him; but you know Him, because He abides with you and shall be in you. I will not leave you as orphans; I am coming to you. Yet a little while and the world beholds Me no longer, but you behold Me; because I live, you also shall live. In that day you will know that I am in My Father, and you in Me, and I in you." In verse 17 the Lord Jesus said that the Spirit of reality would be with the disciples, and then in verse 18 he said, "I am coming to you." While He was speaking, He was already coming. His going was His coming. The day of His coming would be the day of resurrection (v. 20). It is as if the Lord were saying, "There is no need for you to worry. You should be happy. I am leaving, but I am coming. Moreover, My coming is to come into you. Now I am in the flesh; for that reason, I can only be among you. As long as I am in the flesh, I can never be in you. Therefore, I need to be transfigured from the flesh into the Spirit. I need to have a change in form. Through death and resurrection I will be transfigured, changed in form from the flesh into the Spirit." It was in this way, by death and resurrection, that Christ became the life-giving Spirit.

THE LORD COMING ON THE DAY OF RESURRECTION TO BREATHE HIMSELF AS THE SPIRIT INTO THE DISCIPLES

After speaking to His disciples, He delivered Himself to the people to be put on the cross where He was crucified to accomplish redemption. The work of redemption was finished (19:30), and He was put into the grave to rest there. Then on the third day He was resurrected from the dead, and on the day of resurrection He came back to the disciples in a very mysterious way. On that evening the doors were shut in the house where the disciples were for fear of the Jews, but suddenly Christ was among them. Even though no one opened the door, He came into the room and told His disciples to touch His resurrected body. He came back in this mysterious way in order to do one thing, that is, to breathe Himself into the disciples. He breathed into the disciples and said to them, "Receive the Holy Spirit." *Spirit* in Greek is *pneuma,* which also means "breath." At that time He was the Holy Breath for His disciples to breathe. It was in this way that Christ came into the disciples. In the Gospel of John there is no record of Christ's ascension to the heavens. From that time on He was continually in the disciples as the Spirit, the Holy Breath.

THE LORD BEING THE SPIRIT WHO GIVES LIFE

The four Gospels tell us that Christ was God as Spirit who became a man as flesh. He lived on this earth for thirty-three and a half years, and at the end of His earthly life He was put on the cross to accomplish redemption. After accomplishing redemption, He was resurrected, and in His resurrection He became the life-giving Spirit. This is not merely my word. It is the word of the Scriptures: "The last Adam became a life-giving Spirit" (1 Cor. 15:45b). Christ became flesh to accomplish redemption, and then He took another step to become the Spirit to impart life into us. We can confirm this by another verse. Second Corinthians 3:17 says, "The Lord is the Spirit." The Lord here is the Lord Jesus Christ, and the Spirit is the One mentioned in verse 6, which says, "The letter kills, but the Spirit gives life." The Lord Christ is the Spirit who gives life.

CHRIST AS THE ALL-INCLUSIVE SPIRIT
BEING THE SPIRIT THAT WAS FROM THE BEGINNING
WITH FURTHER ELEMENTS ADDED TO HIM

From the beginning, Christ was God, and God is Spirit. Then God as Spirit became a man to die on the cross to bear our sins and accomplish redemption. After this, He was resurrected, and in and by resurrection He became the life-giving Spirit. What then is the difference between the Spirit that was from the beginning and the life-giving Spirit? Are they two Spirits or one? We may illustrate the answer in the following way. Originally, I may have a cup of plain water, but if I gradually pour some juice into it, followed by some milk, tea, honey, and a little salt, eventually I will have a wonderful drink. It is still the water I had originally, but now there is a difference. At first it was purely, plainly, and uniquely water. Now it is still water but with certain elements added to it. Christ as Spirit in eternity was the "plain water," but the life-giving Spirit has further elements added to Him, including incarnation, crucifixion, resurrection, and ascension.

The life-giving Spirit is still the original Spirit, but many wonderful elements have been added to Him. Without crucifixion, redemption, resurrection, and ascension the original Spirit could not come into man. It was not until Christ accomplished redemption, passing through incarnation, crucifixion, resurrection, and ascension that He came into man. How wonderful this is! Now Christ as God is the all-inclusive Spirit with redemption, incarnation, crucifixion, resurrection, and ascension.

IN THE BOOK OF ACTS
THE WONDERFUL ALL-INCLUSIVE SPIRIT
SPREADING TO PRODUCE THE BODY OF CHRIST

Christ as the last Adam became a life-giving Spirit with many wonderful elements added to Him. This is the Spirit in the book of Acts who was spreading to produce the Body of Christ. In the Acts this wonderful Spirit is no longer only the Spirit of God. Acts 16:6-7 says, "And they passed through the region of Phrygia and Galatia, having been forbidden by the Holy Spirit to speak the word in Asia. And when they had come to Mysia, they tried to go into Bithynia, yet the Spirit of Jesus did not allow them." In the Acts the Spirit of God, the Holy Spirit, has become the Spirit of Jesus, who is Christ Himself. It is through the spreading of this wonderful all-inclusive Spirit that the church, the Body of Christ, came into existence.

We need a new understanding, comprehension, and view of all the matters in the book of Acts. What is taking place in this book is the spreading of Jesus as the wonderful Spirit to produce the Body of Christ, which is the church. If we consider this book and the churches in the early days with this point of view, we will have a new understanding. This wonderful Christ mingled Himself with many human beings, including Peter, John, James, Paul, Timothy, and thousands of believers in the early days. All the believers in the Acts were joined to Christ and made one with Christ as the Spirit.

CHRIST AS THE LIFE-GIVING SPIRIT MINGLING
WITH OUR HUMAN SPIRIT TO BE ONE SPIRIT

As we have seen, 1 Corinthians 15:45 tells us that the last Adam became a life-giving Spirit, and 2 Corinthians 3:17 says that the Lord is the Spirit. In addition, 1 Corinthians 6:17 says, "He who is joined to the Lord is one spirit." I hope that you will keep all three of these verses in mind. Here we have Christ as the Spirit in our human spirit, and these two spirits are mingled as one. Christ today is not only the Holy Spirit or the Spirit of God but also the life-giving Spirit, the Spirit who gives life with many wonderful elements added to Him, including incarnation for redemption, crucifixion, resurrection, ascension, and even His enthronement, headship, and lordship. This Spirit comes into our spirit, and these two spirits become one. This oneness is the reality of the church, the church life, and the building up of the Body of Christ. In the early days Peter, Paul, and all of the apostles lived and worked in this oneness. In other words, they lived and worked in this Spirit, that is, in the mingled spirit—Christ as the life-giving Spirit mingled with our human spirit to be one spirit. Now after the book of Acts we have this wonderful mingled spirit in the Epistles.

The foregoing is the foundation and preparation to consider the twenty-two Epistles from Romans through the book of Revelation. In these books we have the definition, explanation, and revelation of this wonderful mingled spirit. In the four Gospels Christ was in the flesh for the purpose of accomplishing redemption. After He accomplished redemption, He was transfigured into another form, the Spirit. Now as the Spirit He comes into our spirit to mingle Himself with our spirit as one in order to be our life, our everything, and our all in all for our experience. In order to experience Christ as our life, our everything, and our all in all in an all-inclusive way, we must realize that today Christ is the wonderful Spirit who indwells our regenerated human spirit. This is the revelation, explanation, and definition found in the twenty-two Epistles. In these books Christ is no longer flesh but Spirit. Redemption has been accomplished, and now He is the Spirit who gives life for us to enjoy, experience, and partake of.

Accordingly, we may summarize our burden for these messages with four sentences: (1) In the Gospels, Christ was life outside of us. (2) In the Acts, Christ is life coming into us. (3) In the Epistles, Christ is life within us to build us up together. (4) In Revelation, Christ is life within us to flow out of us for eternity. This is the revelation of the entire New Testament. All of these matters are contained in one fact, that is, that Christ as the life-giving Spirit mingles Himself with our human spirit to be one spirit.

CHAPTER TWO

THE SPIRIT OF LIFE AND OF SONSHIP
IN ROMANS

Scripture Reading: Rom. 1:1, 3-4; 5:10-11, 17; 6:4; 7:6; 8:2, 4-6, 9-10, 14-16, 23, 26-30; 12:11; 14:17

Romans, the first Epistle, is a very basic book. As we have seen, the four Gospels present Christ as the Head, and the Acts shows us the spreading of the Head, which is His Body, the church composed of many members. Romans tells us how these members come into existence that they may be composed as the Body of Christ. This book gives us a clear picture, showing us that all the members of the Body originally were sinners under God's condemnation. Then these sinners were redeemed, being justified by faith in Christ through His redemption.

BEING SAVED IN LIFE BY CHRIST
AS THE LIFE-GIVING SPIRIT

Only through the first part of chapter 5 of Romans is the justification of sinners covered. After justification there is something deeper and further that is accomplished, not by the death of Christ but by His life. Verse 10 of chapter 5 says, "If we, being enemies, were reconciled to God through the death of His Son, much more we will be saved in His life, having been reconciled." *Were reconciled* is in the past tense, but *will be saved* is in the future tense. Reconciliation by the death of Christ has been accomplished already, but salvation by His life is still going on. We have been reconciled by His death, and now by His life we are being saved. Not only are we saved in His life, but verse 17 goes on to say that we can reign as kings in this life. Following this, 6:4 says that we

walk in the newness of this life, and 7:6 says that we serve
God in newness of spirit. Having been reconciled to God, we
will more and more be saved in His life, reign as kings in this
life, walk in newness of life, and serve in newness of spirit.

Life, the Spirit of Life, the Spirit of God, the Spirit of Christ, and Christ Himself

Romans 6:4 speaks of newness of life, and 7:6 of newness
of spirit. It seems that life and spirit are two things, but chapter 8 puts these two together. Verse 2 uses the title *the Spirit
of life,* and verse 10 says, "If Christ is in you, though the body
is dead because of sin, the spirit is life because of righteousness." Romans mentions life, then spirit, then the Spirit of
life. We should not think that spirit and life are two separate
things. Rather, these two are one. The Spirit is the Spirit of
life, and our spirit is life. To be saved by His life means that
we are saved by the Spirit of life.

Verses 9 through 11 tell us who this Spirit of life is. These
verses say, "You are not in the flesh, but in the spirit, if
indeed the Spirit of God dwells in you. Yet if anyone does not
have the Spirit of Christ, he is not of Him. But if Christ is in
you, though the body is dead because of sin, the spirit is life
because of righteousness. And if the Spirit of the One who
raised Jesus from the dead dwells in you, He who raised
Christ from the dead will also give life to your mortal bodies
through His Spirit who indwells you." According to this context, the Spirit of life is the Spirit of God, the Spirit of God is
the Spirit of Christ, and the Spirit of Christ is Christ Himself.
Moreover, this Christ is in us. We should underline or highlight this short phrase, *Christ is in you,* in verse 10.

In order to read the Bible in the best way, we sometimes
should pick the important words in a passage, write them on
a separate piece of paper, and carefully consider them. All the
above phrases in Romans are very meaningful. First we have
life, then *spirit, the Spirit of life, the Spirit of God, the Spirit
of Christ,* and finally *Christ.* The spirit is life, the Spirit is the
Spirit of life, the Spirit of life is the Spirit of God, the Spirit of
God is the Spirit of Christ, and the Spirit of Christ is Christ

Himself. Eventually, Christ Himself is life (John 14:6; Col. 3:4).

The Spirit of the Son of God for Our Sonship

Romans 8:14-15 says, "For as many as are led by the Spirit of God, these are sons of God. For you have not received a spirit of slavery bringing you into fear again, but you have received a spirit of sonship in which we cry, Abba, Father!" The spirit of sonship is our regenerated human spirit mingled with the Spirit of the Son of God. Sonship is the reality of being a son; thus, the spirit of sonship is the spirit of the reality of being a son. Verse 16 says, "The Spirit Himself witnesses with our spirit that we are children of God." The Spirit of the Son of God witnesses with our spirit that we are the sons of God.

The Firstfruits (Foretaste) of the Spirit

Verse 23 says that with this Spirit of life and of sonship there are the firstfruits, which are a foretaste, just as the firstfruits of an orchard are the foretaste of the harvest. *The firstfruits of the Spirit* indicates that the Spirit of life, the Spirit for our sonship whom we enjoy, is the foretaste and not yet the full taste of our full enjoyment of God. While someone is cooking in the kitchen, before she brings the meal to the dining table, she may taste a little of what she is making. This is a foretaste. Later the full taste will be on the table. Today we are enjoying the Spirit of life and the Spirit for our sonship very much, but even this is only a foretaste. In the future we will have the full taste of the Spirit. In addition, verse 26 says that the Spirit helps us by interceding, and in verse 29 it is the Spirit that conforms us to the image of the Son of God.

All of the above items are included in the one phrase *saved in His life*. To be saved in His life is to be saved in Christ Himself as the life-giving Spirit (1 Cor. 15:45b). The first part of Romans tells us that Christ redeemed us on the cross. Now the middle part of this book tells us that this very redeeming Christ today is within us. "Christ is in you" (8:10). The One who died on the cross to redeem us is now within us. In the past He was on the cross for redemption, but now He is within us for life as the Spirit. Now the redeeming Christ is one with the redeemed sinners. He is in us redeemed ones as our life, the life-giving Spirit, to do many wonderful things for our salvation.

We must be very clear that the Christ in Romans is one with us because He is in us. If Christ had not been made flesh, He could not have died on the cross for our sins as the Lamb of God. He needed to become flesh to be the Lamb of God. If Christ were not the life-giving Spirit, He could not be within us. Today Christ is the life-giving Spirit within us to be our life. In Romans 8 this Spirit is called the Spirit of life, the Spirit of God, the Spirit of Christ, and the Spirit mingled with our spirit to be a spirit of sonship.

THE FOURFOLD WORK OF THE SPIRIT OF LIFE IN ROMANS

The Liberating Spirit

According to the book of Romans, the Spirit of life is doing a fourfold work within us, a work of four aspects. First, the Spirit of life liberates us; that is, He sets us free. Romans 8:2 says, "The law of the Spirit of life has freed me in Christ Jesus from the law of sin and of death." The Spirit of life within us today is liberating us all the time. Christians speak of identification with the death of Christ according to Romans 6. Then they learn to reckon that they are dead (vv. 6, 11), believing that it is by this reckoning that they will be freed from sin. However, this does not work. Our liberation is not in our reckoning; it is in the Spirit of life. When we walk in the Spirit of life, we are freed. There is no need merely to try to identify with the death of Christ or reckon that we are dead. More than thirty years ago I reckoned in this way very much. Eventually, I found out that this simply does not work. Liberation is not in identification or in reckoning but in the Spirit of life.

Moreover, liberation is not in any kind of doctrine. It is not even in the doctrine of the Spirit of life. It is not doctrine or teaching that liberates us. Rather, it is the Spirit of life Himself. We must walk and have our being in the Spirit of life. Whether or not someone knows this doctrine, as long as he is in the Spirit of life, he is freed. We may compare this to electricity. Whether or not someone knows the power of electricity, if he simply touches the electricity, he will be burned. It is not knowledge that liberates us; it is this Spirit of life. Therefore, we need to pray, not that the Lord would liberate us but pray ourselves into the liberation, that is, to pray ourselves into the liberating Spirit. The Spirit of life liberates us from every kind of bondage. When we are in the Spirit of life, we are released.

The Delivering Spirit

Second, the Spirit of life is the delivering Spirit. To be delivered is different from being liberated. On the one hand, we are bound, and on the other hand, we are fallen. Because we are bound, we need liberation, but because we are fallen, we need deliverance. To be delivered is to be saved from the fall. In one sense we have been saved already, but in another sense we are still in the process of being saved. Even up to the present time I still need to be saved. Many times I realize that there is still the element of the fall in my motives, thinking, and feeling. My way of thinking, my mentality, still needs to be delivered from the fall. Also, our physical bodies need deliverance from the fall. We have been saved in our spirit, but we still need to be saved in our soul and in our body.

Romans 5:10 says, "We will be saved in His life, having been reconciled." If we walk in the Spirit of life, all day—even every hour—we will have the sense that we are being saved. In our emotion, in the way we love, and in our conversation there is the element of the fall. Simply consider our attitude. If we are in the Spirit of life and in the light, we will realize how much deliverance we need concerning our attitude. The element of the fall still remains in our attitude, motives, intention, thinking, loving, hating, decisions, and in many other matters. Although many things may not seem wrong, there still may be the element of the fall in them. If we are in the Spirit of life, we will have a deep conviction that in all these matters we need more and more deliverance.

It is not simply a matter of being set free from besetting sins, such as a bad temper. Even within our good temper there is still the element of the fall. We all need to be delivered from our good temper. We truly need deliverance! We need to be delivered out of our temper, disposition, way of thinking, way of loving, way of hating, and many items. Throughout the day, whenever I pray, I spend more time to confess to the Lord than to ask the Lord to do something for me. Whenever I am in the Spirit of life, there is an ever-deepening conviction within me that I need deliverance. The Spirit of life liberates and delivers.

The Sanctifying Spirit

Third, as the Spirit liberates and delivers, He also sanctifies. In the book of Romans to be sanctified means to be saturated through transformation with all that God is (6:19, 22; 12:2). Originally we were worldly; we were common without anything of God. However, now God has come into us, and our whole being is being permeated and saturated with God. In this way we are becoming holy; that is, we are sanctified by being saturated with God. This is the correct meaning of sanctification. The Spirit of life not only liberates us from bondage and delivers us from the fall but also saturates us with God.

Certain Christian teachers have taught that to be sanctified is to be set free from sin. This is not the proper meaning of sanctification. In Romans, sanctification is to be saturated with God. Thus, sanctification equals transformation in 12:2, which says, "Be transformed by the renewing of the mind." To be sanctified is to be transformed by being saturated with God's divine nature. A cup of plain water may be clean, but it is colorless. However, if I permeate the water with orange juice, it becomes orange. This is an illustration of the proper meaning of sanctification. Even if we are clean and pure, we are still not holy. To be clean and pure is one thing, but to be holy is another. To be holy is to be sanctified, to be saturated with God.

The Glorifying Spirit

Eventually the Spirit of life will glorify us (8:30). On the negative side, the Spirit of life within us sets us free and delivers us, and on the positive side, He glorifies us through sanctification and transformation. Eventually He will saturate us with and bring us into the glory of God, not in an objective way but in a very subjective way. We may illustrate glorification with electric lights. All the lights in our meeting room are "glorified" with electricity. We may say that they are saturated with electricity until they shine in the glory of electricity. One day the Spirit of life will saturate us with the glory of God to the extent that we will be glorified in His glory. The Spirit of life liberates, delivers, sanctifies, and eventually glorifies us.

THE WORK OF THE SPIRIT OF THE SON OF GOD FOR OUR SONSHIP

The Witnessing Spirit

The Spirit of the Son of God for our sonship also carries out a work in five aspects. First, this Spirit witnesses with our spirit that we are the children of God (v. 16). Even when we are fallen and backsliding, the Spirit within us always tells us that we are a child of God. Many young Christians go to places where they should not go. While they are there, however, something witnesses, "You are a child of God; you should not be here." Often while we are dressing, once again there is something within us witnessing, "As a child of God, you should not wear this kind of clothing." This is the Spirit of the Son of God for our sonship witnessing with our spirit deep within that we are the children of God.

The Leading Spirit

Second, the Spirit is always leading and guiding us. Verse 14 says, "For as many as are led by the Spirit of God, these are sons of God." Many times the young brothers and sisters have come to ask me what they should do. Almost every time I do not answer directly. Rather, I tell them, "You already know. Why are you coming to me?" Sometimes they argue and say, "No, I do not know." I answer, "You do not know in your mind, but deep within your spirit you do know." We may argue in our mind, but there is something deeper that confirms. The Spirit of the Son for our sonship leads us all the time.

The Interceding Spirit

Third, this Spirit helps us in our interceding (vv. 26-27). The Spirit of the Son is a Spirit of intercession. He witnesses, leads, guides, and prays for us within. There is someone within us always praying for us. If we do not know what He intends and do not have the words to utter, He still groans within us. We all need to learn how to groan. Many times groaning is the best prayer. We should pray not only with plain words. Many times we need to pray with groans that cannot be uttered.

The Conforming Spirit

Fourth, because the Spirit is the reality of sonship, He is doing a work to conform us to the image of the Son of God (v. 29). This makes us true sons, sons not merely in name and not only in life and nature but also in image, appearance, and reality. He makes us the real sons of God by conforming us to the image of the Son of God. This Spirit is doing a great work within us, nearly all of which is mentioned in one chapter, Romans 8. That is why Romans 8 may be considered the greatest chapter in the entire Bible.

The Building Spirit

The fifth aspect pertains not only to the Spirit of the Son for our sonship but also to the Spirit of life. As we have seen, the Spirit of life liberates, delivers, sanctifies, and eventually glorifies us, and the Spirit for our sonship witnesses, leads, helps us to pray, and conforms us to the image of the Son of God. All this work is with one aim, which is to build us up. Although the phrase *build up* is not in the book of Romans, the thought and concept of building is found in chapter 12. All the sons of God are the members of Christ, and all these members need to be built up and coordinated together (vv. 4-5). This mutual membership and relatedness is the ultimate work of the Spirit of life and the Spirit of the Son of God for our sonship. He frees, delivers, sanctifies, and glorifies us, and He witnesses within, leads us, prays for us, and conforms us to the image of Christ that we may be the real sons of God.

Then we become the living, true, proper members of the Body of Christ, and the Spirit of life and of sonship builds us up together. We become members one of another and are joined and knit together by the work of this Spirit. This is the inner working of the life-giving Spirit within us. Through all this inward working we become members, we are built up as the living Body of Christ, and we have the proper church life described in chapter 12.

The Spirit of life and of sonship is the Spirit of God, the Spirit of Christ, and Christ Himself as the life-giving Spirit. It is by this Spirit that we enjoy Christ as our life, and it is in this life that we are being saved, including being set free, delivered, sanctified, and glorified, sharing with His witnessing, being led, helped in our interceding, conformed to the image of the Son of God, and built up together. To be saved includes many items. Eventually, sinners become the glorious sons of God, sons of God in glory, who are built up together as the Body of Christ. All these items are included in the divine salvation by Christ being life to us, and they are worked out within us by the life-giving Spirit. Today the church needs more messages telling people how much we need to experience Christ as the wonderful, all-inclusive Spirit of life.

CHAPTER THREE

ENJOYING GOD, REIGNING IN LIFE, WALKING IN NEWNESS OF LIFE, AND SERVING IN NEWNESS OF SPIRIT

Scripture Reading: Rom. 5:10-11, 17; 9:5; 6:4; 7:6, 25; 8:2, 4, 16; 12:2, 11; 14:17

ENJOYING GOD AND BOASTING IN HIM

Romans 5:10-11 says, "If we, being enemies, were reconciled to God through the death of His Son, much more we will be saved in His life, having been reconciled, and not only so, but also boasting in God through our Lord Jesus Christ, through whom we have now received the reconciliation." To boast in God is to glory in God and enjoy God. Now God is our portion, and we enjoy Him. Not only do we need to be reconciled to God, to be saved from many negative things, but we also need to enjoy God positively. Verse 11 speaks of reconciliation, rather than atonement. Atonement, or expiation, is an Old Testament concept; it does not belong in the New Testament. Redemption is much better than atonement. In the Old Testament, before the accomplishment of redemption, people needed atonement, but because redemption has now been accomplished, there is no further need of atonement. Now we have God as our portion and enjoyment, and we enjoy Him and glory and boast in Him.

REIGNING IN LIFE

Verse 17 says that we will "reign in life through the One, Jesus Christ." In the book of Romans, we enjoy God and we reign as kings in life. This is not merely to overcome our temper or deal with besetting sins in a miserable way. This is to reign as kings gloriously. We enjoy God, boast in Him, and reign in life.

The very God whom we enjoy, in whom we boast and glory, and who is our portion, is Christ. Verse 5 of chapter 9 says, "Christ, who is God over all, blessed forever." Christ our portion is the very God who is blessed forever. Likewise, Christ is the life in which we reign. Moreover, He is the life-giving Spirit, and He is within our spirit (8:2, 16; 1 Cor. 15:45; 2 Tim. 4:22). Christ is our God and our life. In this God we boast, glory, and joy, and in this life we reign as kings, ruling over all things. This is the revelation in the book of Romans.

WALKING IN NEWNESS OF LIFE
AND SERVING IN NEWNESS OF SPIRIT

Verse 4 of chapter 6 says, "Walk in newness of life." Since Christ is our life, to walk in newness of life is to walk in the newness of Christ. Then 7:6 says, "Serve in newness of spirit." We walk in newness of life and serve in newness of spirit. *Spirit* in verse 6 is our human spirit, and Christ today is in our spirit. We need to serve in the newness of the spirit in which Christ dwells.

THE SPIRIT OF LIFE

Chapter 7 brings us back from our deliverance by life to the old man, the self, the evil "I." Verse 25 says, "So then with the mind I myself serve the law of God, but with the flesh, the law of sin." The phrase *with the mind I myself* sounds like ugly music. We should compare the words *mind, I,* and *myself* to *boast in God, reign in life, walk in newness of life,* and *serve in newness of spirit*. With the mind, I, and myself there is no joy or newness, but only ugliness. Chapter 7 is a deep valley, but after the valley chapter 8 is the glorious mountain peak. Verse 2 of chapter 8 begins, "For the law of the Spirit of life." This is the unique verse in the Bible that uses the term *the Spirit of life*. Many Christians today emphasize the Spirit of power, but not many consider the Spirit of life. What we need is not so much the Spirit of power but the Spirit of life. We are not motorcars that need more power. Rather, we are grains of wheat that need life. Our power must be the power of life, the power of resurrection, not a power apart from life.

WALKING ACCORDING TO THE SPIRIT AND BEING RENEWED IN OUR MIND

Verse 4 says, "That the righteous requirement of the law might be fulfilled in us, who do not walk according to the flesh but according to the spirit," and verse 6 continues, "For the mind set on the flesh is death, but the mind set on the spirit is life and peace." Chapters 7 through 12 show us a process with respect to the mind. First, 7:25 says, "With the mind I myself serve the law of God." This is an endeavoring, a striving, which does not avail for us. Here the mind is the means to serve with our self. No doubt, this is the independent, old mind. Then in chapter 8 the mind is turned in the right direction; it is turned to the spirit and set on the spirit. Finally, 12:2 says, "Do not be fashioned according to this age, but be transformed by the renewing of the mind." Here the mind is in the process of being renewed. Originally it was the old, independent mind, but from this time onward it is being renewed to fulfill the purpose of the spirit. Now the mind can be used by the spirit as its organ.

THE KEY POINT OF THE ENTIRE CHRISTIAN LIFE

The redeeming Christ today is within us as the life-giving Spirit. On the cross He was the redeeming Lamb of God, and now in our spirit He is the life-giving Spirit. The Lamb is for redemption, and the Spirit is for life. Redemption was accomplished outside of us, on the cross, but life is something inside of us, in our spirit. The key point of the Christian life is that Christ is in our spirit and that this wonderful Christ is the all-inclusive life-giving Spirit. God, man, crucifixion, incarnation, resurrection, ascension, glory, power, life, and everything are all in Him, and He is within us.

Man is of three parts—spirit, soul, and body. Originally God created man with a body, not with the flesh, but because Satan came into man's body, the body was ruined, corrupted, and poisoned by Satan and changed in nature to become the flesh. Similarly, within the mind is the self. The mind is the leading part of the soul and represents the soul. This is why some translators of the New Testament render the Greek word for *soul* as *mind,* as in Philippians 1:27 (KJV, NASB). When we were saved, Christ came into our spirit as our life. In our body there is Satan as sin, making it the flesh, and in our mind there is the self. However, in our spirit we have Christ as life and everything.

The first three chapters of Romans portray man as living in the flesh. Before we were saved, we were either Jews or Gentiles living all the time in the flesh to do sinful things. After someone is saved, he may not be clear in his experience that he should not try to live by himself, so chapter 7 is a record of a person living by himself, serving the law of God with the mind and the self. This is the record of a good man. Both the man living in the flesh sinfully in Romans 1—3 and the man living in the soul morally in Romans 7 are wrong. Instead, we need to live in the spirit, neither sinfully nor morally but spiritually, because Christ today is the life-giving Spirit who lives in our spirit. He as the Spirit mingles Himself with our spirit, so now these two spirits are one (1 Cor. 6:17). This is the key point of the entire Christian life.

WALKING IN AND ACCORDING TO OUR MINGLED SPIRIT

The Spirit has a long history and includes many elements. He is the true God, the Triune God, and He is also the real man. In Him also are incarnation, human living, human suffering, crucifixion, resurrection with the resurrection power, ascension, glorification, and enthronement. All the accomplishments and attainments of the God-man are included in the Spirit. The human spirit also is not simple. Our spirit was created by God to receive God Himself. In the fall it was deadened but was still preserved by God. Now Christ has come into it to make it alive, to regenerate and uplift it. Our spirit is regenerated, uplifted, and indwelt by Christ. Thus, both the Spirit and our spirit have a long story, and now these two spirits are mingled together as one spirit. This is the wonderful spirit mentioned in the Epistles. We must learn all these matters and minister them to people in every place.

We need to walk in and according to this wonderful spirit

(Rom. 8:4). When we walk according to this spirit, all things are ours. There is no need to seek after victory, because when we walk in this spirit, victory is ours. In fact, there is even no need of victory. We only need victory when we have enemies. In the spirit, however, there is no enemy. In the New Jerusalem we will have no enemies, so there will be no need of victory. Likewise, in our spirit there are no problems, so there is no need of solutions. As long as we are in this wonderful spirit, everything is all right. Moreover, the supply is here. Whatever we need is in our spirit. If we need light, here is the light. If we need comfort, joy, peace, rest, power, or patience, all these and something more are in our spirit. This is why the entire Bible eventually brings us to this point, stressing that we should walk in the spirit, live in the spirit, pray in the spirit, love our brothers in the spirit, have fellowship in the spirit, and do everything in the spirit. When we are in this spirit, everything is wonderful. All the problems are not only solved but are gone altogether.

When we live in the flesh, everything is "smoggy," but in the spirit we are free from all smog. Our spirit is "smog free," and there are no problems there. In our flesh there are many negative involvements. When we live in the flesh, we are involved with Satan, and Satan is related to the world. Likewise, when we live in the self, in the mind, we have more complications. We should no longer live in our self, trying to serve the law of God with the mind by ourselves. We must no longer say, "With the mind I myself serve." Rather, we must pay our full attention to walking in the spirit, because this is where the wonderful Christ is today.

THE PRACTICAL WAY TO SET OUR MIND ON THE SPIRIT

In order to walk according to the spirit, we first need to set our mind on the spirit. In other words, we need to turn our mind to the spirit. We are always used to setting our mind in the other direction, toward the flesh. When we set our mind on the flesh, we have death, but when we set our mind on the spirit, we have life and peace. Life is the strength to energize us, and peace affords us enjoyment. Whenever we turn our mind to the spirit, we are immediately strengthened and in the enjoyment of Christ. Christ is life, and He is peace. This means that when we set our mind on the spirit, we have Christ as life strengthening us, nourishing us, and being our enjoyment.

We need to see the way to put this into practice. The subtle tactic of the enemy is often to attract our mind to something outward, tempting us to set our mind on something other than the spirit. If we have a bad temper, Satan will utilize this temper, tempting us to pay attention to our temper. Then we will consider how to overcome our temper and conduct ourselves so as not to lose our temper. This means that spontaneously and automatically we are setting our mind on our temper instead of on the spirit. Thousands of items are utilized by Satan to tempt us to turn from the spirit to something else. The right and best way is to forget about all these things. We should forget about our temper and a thousand other matters, not pay any attention to them, and simply turn our mind to the spirit.

I have been a Christian for more than forty years, and for many of these years I had not yet discovered this glorious way. We need to forget about our weaknesses, shortcomings, temper, and other failures and pay attention to nothing other than the spirit. All the time we simply need to turn our mind to the spirit and set it on the spirit. If we are short of patience or humility, Satan will constantly tempt us to pay attention to these things. However, the more we set our mind on patience and humility, the more we will not have them. We need to forget about humility and patience and always consider the spirit, pay attention to the spirit, set our mind on the spirit, and turn our mind to the spirit.

To set our mind on the spirit means that we remain in the spirit. Then we will walk, move, do things, and speak things according to the spirit in which we remain. This way is very clear and simple. If we act, speak, move, work, and have our being in the spirit, remaining in the spirit, we will be transcendent. We will be in the heavens, and all the enemies will be under our feet. Then when there are no more enemies, there will be nothing further to overcome. Spontaneously we will enjoy the Lord, and we will fulfill the righteous requirements of the law. We will unconsciously and unintentionally fulfill everything that the law demands, because we will surpass the requirements of the law. We will be in the spirit, and in our spirit there will be no problems to overcome.

BEING BURNING IN SPIRIT

Romans 12:11 says, "Do not be slothful in zeal, but be burning in spirit, serving the Lord." What we need is not to do many things but rather to be burning in spirit. This requires that we pray to stay in the presence of the Lord. First, we need to set our mind on the spirit, and second, we must walk according to the spirit. Third, our spirit must be burning. We need to be on fire with the Lord as the fire. We should pray to spend more and more time in the presence of the Lord. If we pray even for half an hour a day, we will be burning. We can compare our spirit to an electric iron. If we leave the iron plugged in for half an hour, it will be burning hot. To be burning in the spirit means that we are on fire in the spirit. The Lord Himself is the consuming fire, the holy and divine fire. Therefore, we need to stay in His presence.

If a Christian prays for an hour and a half daily, he will be spiritually "crazy." Someone who prays for an hour and a half cannot be cold, clear, and clever. All the clever Christians are cold ones. To be too clever and clear means that we are too cold. When we are burning in spirit, we are not very clear; rather, we are "God-fools," fools because of Christ (1 Cor. 4:10; 2 Cor. 5:13). When we are cold, we always know how to count the cost, but when we are burning in the spirit, we are foolish, forgetting about the loss. We all need to be burning. Judas, who betrayed the Lord Jesus, was very clear. He was the best accountant, calculating the cost, and eventually he calculated thirty pieces of silver (Matt. 26:6-9, 14-15). This kind of person has not only a cold spirit but also a dead spirit. When our spirit is living and burning, we will not be clear to count the cost.

In a certain sense, Christians should be foolish. If we have never done something foolish for the Lord, if we have never been beside ourselves, we have never been a good Christian (2 Cor. 5:13). A good Christian, at least sometimes, needs to be

beside himself. We need to be burning in the spirit; we must
not be so cold. There are many wonderful stories of people
who were so burned by the Lord that they did something
"foolish" for Him.

BEING JOYFUL IN THE SPIRIT

Romans 14:17 says, "For the kingdom of God is not eating
and drinking, but righteousness and peace and joy in the Holy
Spirit." Righteousness is toward ourselves, peace is toward
others, and joy is toward God in the Holy Spirit. We need to be
joyful in the spirit. A Christian must be a joyful person. This
does not mean that our circumstances will be wonderful. It
may actually mean that we are in a "furnace," like the three
friends of Daniel (Dan. 3:19-20, 25). They were in the burning
furnace, but they were still joyful. Our surroundings and circumstances may be miserable, but we ourselves must be
joyful. If between us and God there is no joy, we are wrong. If
we are right with God, there will always be joy, even if we are
suffering. When the apostles Paul and Silas were put into
prison, their surroundings were terrible, but they were joyful
(Acts 16:23-25). To their feeling they were not in the jail but
in God. To them, the jail was simply the representative of God,
and they were in Him (Eph. 4:1). Therefore, they were joyful.

If we are not burning and joyful, we must be wrong in
some way. When we are burning in our spirit and joyful in the
Holy Spirit, we enjoy God, reign as kings in life, walk in newness of life, and serve in newness of spirit. In our service
we will not give people a feeling of oldness. Rather, in our
service and ministry we will always give others a feeling of
freshness and newness. Our message may be the same, but
the feeling will be new and fresh.

THE REVELATION IN THE BOOK OF ROMANS

Our being new and fresh requires that we set our mind on
our spirit, walk in the spirit and according to the spirit, be
burning in spirit, and be joyful in the Holy Spirit. In this way
we will boast in God and enjoy Him as our portion. We will
spontaneously reign in life as kings, walk in newness of
life, and serve in newness of spirit. This is what the book of

Romans tells us. Then all the matters mentioned in the last portion of this book, from chapters 12 through 16, are the things we will enjoy in our spirit. When we enjoy God in a burning and joyful spirit, we have all these matters.

The book of Romans is of three sections. The first part tells us that we are justified in Christ, and the second part tells us to walk in the spirit. Then the last part tells us that as we walk in the spirit, we become related with one another to be the living Body of Christ expressing Him to the fullest degree. The Christ who was on the cross as the redeeming Lamb is within us today as the life-giving Spirit, mingling Himself with our human spirit. Now He and we are one spirit. Therefore, we must always regard this spirit, set our mind on the spirit, live and walk according to this spirit, and pray in the spirit, remaining there to spend time in the presence of the Lord so that our spirit will be burning and full of joy. We will enjoy the Lord, reign in life, walk in newness of life, and serve in newness of spirit. Then our whole being will be transformed by the renewing of the mind, and we will be conformed to the image of the Son of God. In this way we will be the real sons of God and the living members of Christ, who are related one with another and built up together as the living Body to express Christ. This is the message of the book of Romans. I look to the Lord that He would have mercy upon us so that we all may see these matters. The key point is that we need to turn to our spirit, remain there, and walk and live according to this spirit. Then all the good things in this book will be worked out.

CHAPTER FOUR

THE LIFE-GIVING SPIRIT
FOR THE BUILDING OF GOD'S HOUSE
IN 1 CORINTHIANS

Scripture Reading: 1 Cor. 1:1-2, 9, 5-7, 22-24, 30; 2:2, 9-16; 3:1-3, 7-13a, 16-17; 6:17, 19; 7:10, 12a, 25, 40; 10:1-4; 12:3-4, 7-13; 15:45b

It is not easy for many Christians to receive the proper light concerning the life-giving Spirit in 1 Corinthians. Even though the apostle presents the Spirit in a particular way, many today are too impressed with the supernatural gifts of the Spirit. Before we get into this book, we need to forget this kind of unbalanced impression. Let us come to this book with a pure understanding. If we put off the "tinted glasses" from our eyes, we will see the pure revelation from the pure Word.

THE ALL-INCLUSIVE CHRIST
BEING OUR UNIQUE PORTION

Let us consider certain important passages from this book. Verses 1 and 2 of chapter 1 say, "Paul, a called apostle of Christ Jesus through the will of God, and Sosthenes the brother, to the church of God which is in Corinth, to those who have been sanctified in Christ Jesus, the called saints, with all those who call upon the name of our Lord Jesus Christ in every place, who is theirs and ours." We should highlight the phrase *theirs and ours*. This means that Christ is both their portion and our portion. Then verse 9 says, "God is faithful, through whom you were called into the fellowship of His Son, Jesus Christ our Lord." Christ is our portion, and God has called us into the fellowship, the enjoyment, of this portion. Verse 30 says, "Of Him you are in Christ Jesus, who became wisdom to us from God: both righteousness and sanctification and redemption." That Christ has been made all these items to us means that He is everything to us. He is our divine portion, and He is all in all to us.

Verses 22 through 24 say, "For indeed Jews require signs and Greeks seek wisdom, but we preach Christ crucified, to Jews a stumbling block, and to Gentiles foolishness, but to those who are called, both Jews and Greeks, Christ the power of God and the wisdom of God." The phrase *but we preach Christ* in verse 23 indicates that signs and wisdom are not Christ. Rather, to certain people they are substitutes for Christ. We do not want to follow the Jews or the Greeks. The Jews require a sign, which is something miraculous, and the Greeks seek after knowledge. Instead, we want to follow the apostles, who preached Christ crucified.

Verses 5 through 7 say, "That in everything you were enriched in Him, in all utterance and all knowledge, even as the testimony of Christ was confirmed in you, so that you do not lack in any gift, eagerly awaiting the revelation of our Lord Jesus Christ." Utterance, knowledge, and gifts may also be substitutes for Christ. These things are good, but all these are not Christ Himself. The Corinthians did not lack any gift, but they were not spiritual men. Rather, they were infants and fleshy (3:1-3). They had all utterance, knowledge, and gifts, but they were short of Christ.

In 1 Corinthians 1 Christ is presented as our all-inclusive portion. He is the wisdom prepared for us by God to be our righteousness in the past, sanctification in the present, and redemption in the future so that He may be our portion and our all in all. Moreover, we have been called by God into the fellowship of this Christ. He is ours, and He is theirs. He is the divine portion allotted by God to every believer. Miracles, signs, wisdom, utterance, knowledge, and gifts may simply be substitutes for Christ. We can be distracted from Christ by all these things that are not Christ Himself. In this chapter Paul stresses that nothing less than the all-inclusive Christ is our portion, not even the good things. Paul confirms this in chapter 2, saying, "For I did not determine to know anything among you except Jesus Christ, and this One crucified" (v. 2).

Paul made the decision not to know anything of signs, miracles, wisdom, utterance, knowledge, or gifts. Instead, he determined to know Jesus Christ and Him crucified.

THE REVEALING, SEARCHING, KNOWING, TEACHING, AND DISCERNING SPIRIT

In chapter 2 Paul gives us the practical way to experience and enjoy Christ by the Spirit. Verses 9 through 14 say, "As it is written, 'Things which eye has not seen and ear has not heard and which have not come up in man's heart; things which God has prepared for those who love Him.' But to us God has revealed them through the Spirit, for the Spirit searches all things, even the depths of God. For who among men knows the things of man, except the spirit of man which is in him? In the same way, the things of God also no one has known except the Spirit of God. But we have received not the spirit of the world but the Spirit which is from God, that we may know the things which have been graciously given to us by God; which things also we speak, not in words taught by human wisdom but in words taught by the Spirit, interpreting spiritual things with spiritual words. But a soulish man does not receive the things of the Spirit of God, for they are foolishness to him and he is not able to know them because they are discerned spiritually." The things that God has given us freely are the things of Christ, including His life, and the depths of God are Christ in many aspects as our enjoyment. *Interpreting spiritual things with spiritual words* in verse 13 is to explain spiritual things by spiritual means. The Spirit explains the spiritual things, the deep things of God concerning Christ, by means of spiritual words.

In these verses five verbs are used to describe how the Spirit works within us related to the things of Christ: *revealed, searches, knows, taught,* and *discerned.* The Spirit of God searches the things of Christ, knows the things of Christ, and reveals and teaches the things of Christ to us, and we discern these things by the Spirit.

Verses 15 continues, "But the spiritual man discerns all things, but he himself is discerned by no one." We need to be spiritual and not soulish. If we are soulish, we cannot understand and receive the things of Christ. To be soulish means to live and to walk in the soul. To be spiritual means to live and walk in the spirit. The way to experience Christ is by the spirit, not by the soul. The deep things of God are Christ Himself, and the things that God has given to us freely are also Christ Himself. We need to experience this Christ in our spirit through the Holy Spirit, because it is the Spirit that searches the things of Christ, knows the things of Christ, and reveals, teaches, and discerns the things of Christ.

Because this Spirit is now in our spirit, we must be in our spirit. If we are soulish and in the soul, we are foolish; we cannot know and receive the things of Christ. We need to live and walk in the spirit and not in the soul. If we live and walk in the soul, we become soulish and natural men, men who cannot receive the things of Christ. It is in the spirit that we contact the Spirit of God who reveals and teaches all the things of Christ to us.

Chapter 2 concludes with verse 16, which says, "For who has known the mind of the Lord and will instruct Him? But we have the mind of Christ." To have the mind of Christ means that our mind is renewed and our soul is transformed. Romans 12:2 says, "Be transformed by the renewing of the mind." As we have seen before, man is of three parts—spirit, soul, and body. The Spirit dwells in our spirit to reveal and teach all the things of Christ to us. Therefore, we need to walk and live in the spirit, not in the soul. When we walk and live in the spirit, we give the free way to Christ to flood us and fill us. From our spirit He will spread into the parts of our soul, which are our mind, emotion, and will. Then our mind will be renewed. It will no longer be the natural mind but the mind of Christ. This is to be transformed in our soul. It is in this way that we experience Christ as our all-inclusive portion.

In 1 Corinthians 1 we have Christ as our portion, and in chapter 2 we have the Spirit as the way, the means, for us to enjoy our portion. Because this Spirit is in our spirit, we need to be spiritual men living and walking in our spirit. In this way we will continually contact the Spirit who reveals and teaches Christ to us. Moreover, as we walk and live in the spirit, the Spirit will take possession of our entire being, and

Christ will have the free way to flood and saturate us. Then all the parts of our soul will be renewed and transformed, and we will enjoy Christ as everything to us.

THE INDWELLING, FEEDING, TRANSFORMING, AND BUILDING SPIRIT

First Corinthians 3:1-3 says, "And I, brothers, was not able to speak to you as to spiritual men, but as to fleshy, as to infants in Christ." In chapter 2 Paul says that we must be spiritual men. If we are soulish, we cannot enjoy Christ. In chapter 3, however, he said that he could not speak to the Corinthians as to spiritual men but as to fleshy. *Fleshy* is a stronger expression than *fleshly*. In chapters 1 through 4 the Corinthians had jealousy, strife, and divisions. All these are fleshly things. In chapters 5 and 6, though, some committed things even more evil. Those who did such things were fleshy, made of the flesh and totally of the flesh. Paul spoke to the Corinthians as to fleshy, because among them there was even one who committed incest with his stepmother. This was to behave not only as soulish or fleshly but as fleshy.

Chapter 3 continues, "I gave you milk to drink, not solid food, for you were not yet able to receive it. But neither yet now are you able, for you are still fleshly. For if there is jealousy and strife among you, are you not fleshly and do you not walk according to the manner of man?" (vv. 2-3). The Corinthian believers, who had received all utterance and knowledge and were lacking in no gift, were short of Christ. They were babyish, soulish, fleshly, and even fleshy.

Verses 7 through 9 say, "So then neither is he who plants anything nor he who waters, but God who causes the growth. Now he who plants and he who waters are one, but each will receive his own reward according to his own labor. For we are God's fellow workers; you are God's cultivated land, God's building." Here Paul says that we are two things, in two aspects. We are God's cultivated land to grow a harvest, and we are also God's building. As the cultivated land we need to grow, and as the building we need to be built up. The house of God is not a house without life; it is a living house, a house that is full of life. Therefore, the building of this house depends on the growth of life. We need not only to be built together but also to grow together.

Verses 10 through 13a say, "According to the grace of God given to me, as a wise master builder I have laid a foundation, and another builds upon it. But let each man take heed how he builds upon it. For another foundation no one is able to lay besides that which is laid, which is Jesus Christ. But if anyone builds upon the foundation gold, silver, precious stones, wood, grass, stubble, the work of each will become manifest." Then verses 16 and 17 continue, "Do you not know that you are the temple of God, and that the Spirit of God dwells in you? If anyone destroys the temple of God, God will destroy him; for the temple of God is holy, and such are you."

According to a careful reading of this chapter, the Holy Spirit today is the Spirit who indwells us to give us the growth in life, transform us into precious materials, and build us up together. Following this, there is the temple of God. Again, this house of God is a living house. It is a building that requires the growth of life. On the one hand, we are the cultivated land of God, and on the other hand, we are the building of God. Therefore, we need to grow. The way to grow is by the Spirit. Then by growing we are transformed into gold, silver, and precious stones. Originally we all were only clay. We were not gold, silver, or precious stones. However, by growing in life we are transformed into these precious materials, and by being transformed we are built up together. The work of the indwelling Spirit is to give us the growth of life, transform us into precious materials, and build us together as the temple of God.

The way the Spirit gives us the growth is by feeding us (v. 2). The Spirit that dwells within us feeds us with Christ either as milk or as solid food. If we are too young or childish, the Spirit knows that He must feed us with Christ as milk. Mothers know that they cannot feed babes with steak. They need to be fed with milk little by little. The apostle Paul fed the Corinthian believers in this way. Growth in life comes not merely from teaching. Growth comes by feeding on something of Christ either as milk or as solid food (Heb. 5:12-14). It is by feeding that we grow, it is by growth in life that we are transformed, and it is by this transformation that we become the precious stones that are good for the building up of the temple of God. In 1 Corinthians 3, therefore, the indwelling Spirit is the feeding Spirit, the transforming Spirit, and the building Spirit.

We must not only know Christ but also feed on Christ. We need to enjoy Christ by eating and drinking Him (John 6:57; 7:37). Then we will grow in life, and it is by this growth that we are gradually transformed into precious materials for the building of God's house. We can see this also in the six parables in Matthew 13. The first four parables deal with the sower who sowed the seed, the seed growing into wheat, the growing mustard seed, and the fine flour from the wheat that becomes bread. All these are related to God's cultivated land that grows something to be blent as fine flour to make a loaf, signifying the Body of Christ. Following this are the parables of the treasure hidden in the field and the pearl hidden in the water. Both the treasure and the pearl are precious materials that are good for the building of God. This indicates that the precious materials come from the transformation of that which grows out of the land.

This growth of life comes from feeding on Christ as our food, our nourishment. We need to feed on Christ day by day. Then we will be nourished to grow, and by this growth we will spontaneously and gradually be transformed into precious materials for the building of God. All this is the work of the indwelling Spirit.

THE SPIRIT JOINED TO OUR SPIRIT
AND OCCUPYING OUR BODY
FOR THE BUILDING OF THE TEMPLE OF GOD

First Corinthians 6:17 reveals something even more wonderful. It is a great matter, not only in the Bible but also in the whole universe. This verse says, "But he who is joined to the Lord is one spirit." Following this, verses 19 and 20 say, "Or do you not know that your body is a temple of the Holy Spirit within you, whom you have from God, and you are not your own? For you have been bought with a price. So then glorify God in your body." This passage states clearly that the

Holy Spirit dwells not only in our spirit but also in our body. Our whole being, not only our spirit but also our body, becomes the temple of God.

This is wonderful, but it requires much work. A fleshly or fleshy person's body cannot be the temple of God. This body must be saturated by the Spirit who dwells in our spirit. The Spirit is in our spirit, and now He wants to spread through our soul to permeate our body. Then even our body will become a part of the divine temple. This is the proper meaning of *glorify God in your body*. To glorify God in our body is to manifest God through our body. Our body, not only our soul, must be under the control of the spirit. When our soul and our body are both under the control of our spirit, the spirit can manifest something of God in our body.

When the Spirit possesses even our body, we are fit to be built up together as the Body of Christ. Romans 12:1 tells us to present our body for the Body of Christ. We need to offer our physical body for the mystical Body of Christ. If we fellowship with the Lord with our spirit and love Him with our heart, but our body is not occupied by the spirit for the Lord's purpose, we cannot realize the Body life. In order to realize the church life, our spirit must be filled with the Holy Spirit, our soul must be transformed by all of its parts being renewed, and our body must be occupied by the Spirit. This means that our entire being—spirit, soul, and body—is taken over by the Spirit. Then it will be easy to be related with the other saints, and we will be in the Body of Christ in a practical way. We need to offer our physical body for the mystical Body of Christ. A spirit to contact the Lord and a heart to love the Lord are not good enough. We also need to offer our body to the Lord as a living sacrifice. Then we will have the Body life, and when we have the Body life, we will truly glorify God in our body.

We fellowship with the Lord, but fellowship is a matter of the spirit. Likewise, we love the Lord, and we set our mind on the spirit, but this is a matter of the heart. Our body, however, may not yet be a living sacrifice for the Body of Christ. Our body needs to be set free from many preoccupations. When we visit certain ones, they sometimes say, "Thank you for your concern. I have been away from the meetings for several months, but I assure you that my heart is with the Lord." Yes, our heart is with the Lord, but what about our body? If our body is not presented for the practical church life, then to say that our heart is with the Lord is to speak a kind of lie wrapped in a truth. If our body does not come, our being is not coming in reality. To say that our heart is in America though our body is in Taiwan simply means we are still in Taiwan. The body is the appearance of a man in reality. If our body is not present, our being cannot be present.

The spirit is in the soul, the soul is in the body, and the body is in time. Therefore, we need to designate time for our body to come to the church life in practicality. If our time is preoccupied, our whole being is occupied. That is why we need to separate out a part of our time for our body to come to the church life. Then when our body comes, our soul comes, and when our soul comes, our spirit comes. The Holy Spirit within us today is working to transform our soul, occupy our body, and separate our time to the Lord. Then we will glorify God in our body by being in the Body of Christ in practicality.

BEING ONE SPIRIT WITH THE LORD
TO SPEAK FOR HIM

First Corinthians 7:10 says, "To the married I charge, not I but the Lord, A wife must not be separated from her husband." When Paul charged, it was not he but the Lord. This is the real oneness with the Lord according to 6:17: "He who is joined to the Lord is one spirit." Then verse 12a of chapter 7 says, "But to the rest I say, I, not the Lord." In verse 10 he says, "Not I but the Lord," while in verse 12 he says, "I, not the Lord." We may be more "spiritual" than the apostle Paul. Today many ministers say in a pretentious way, "The Lord gives me the burden to speak to you." Sometimes we do need to have the boldness to say, "I charge, not I but the Lord," but sometimes we also need to say, "I, not the Lord."

Verse 25 continues, "Now concerning virgins I have no commandment of the Lord, but I give my opinion as one who has been shown mercy by the Lord to be faithful." It seems that if someone does not have a commandment from the Lord, he should not speak. However, this chapter of 1 Corinthians is a portrait of a person at the peak of spirituality. On the one hand, he could say that when he speaks, it is the Lord speaking. On the other hand, he recognizes that although his speaking is not a commandment from the Lord, he could still give his judgment, concept, or opinion. This is genuine spirituality. Here is a person who has been occupied by the Lord, taken over by the Lord, saturated and permeated with the Lord, and mingled with the Lord. When he spoke, whether as from the Lord directly or simply in giving his opinion, he was one with the Lord. Even when he did not have the feeling that he had the Lord's direct commandment, he could still speak something of the Lord.

Verse 40 concludes, "But she is more blessed if she so remains, according to my opinion; but I think that I also have the Spirit of God." Paul gave his opinion, but he still thought that he had the Spirit of God. The more spiritual we are, the less assurance we will have. When we say, "I am sure that I am in the spirit," it is doubtful that we are in the spirit. Rather, we should say, "I do not know, and I am not clear. This may be my opinion, judgment, and concept. I am not sure, but I think that I have the Spirit of God."

Paul's word in chapter 7 is recognized as the word of God. Brother Watchman Nee once pointed out to us that this is the climax of spirituality. A truly spiritual person must be like this. We must not say, "Because I am full of the Spirit and under the power of the Spirit, what I am speaking to you must be of the Lord." Such a speaking does not appear in the New Testament. On the contrary, here is a person saying, "I say, I, not the Lord...I have no commandment of the Lord, but I give my opinion...But I think that I also have the Spirit of God." Nevertheless, whatever he spoke was the word of God, because by this time the apostle Paul was a person truly joined to the Lord as one spirit. He was so occupied by the Lord, mingled with the Lord, and thoroughly saturated with the Lord that even his concept and judgment were something from the Lord.

This is the message of 1 Corinthians. Yes, in chapters 12 and 14 there is the matter of speaking in tongues. However, the church today needs chapter 7 more than the tongues in chapters 12 and 14. We need not merely the outward manifestation of the gifts but the inward mingling of the Lord with us as one. Even when we do not have the feeling or assurance that what we speak is something from the Lord, eventually what we speak is of the Lord because we are saturated with Him and one with Him in reality. "He who is joined to the Lord is one spirit" (6:17).

CHRIST BEING OUR SPIRITUAL FOOD, SPIRITUAL DRINK, AND SPIRITUAL ROCK

Chapter 10 begins, "For I do not want you to be ignorant, brothers, that all our fathers were under the cloud, and all passed through the sea; and all were baptized unto Moses in the cloud and in the sea; and all ate the same spiritual food, and all drank the same spiritual drink; for they drank of a spiritual rock which followed them, and the rock was Christ" (vv. 1-4). This chapter shows us that today Christ is everything to us. He is not physical food, a psychological drink, or a material rock. Rather, He is our spiritual food, spiritual drink, and spiritual rock. Therefore, we need to enjoy Him, experience Him, feed on Him, drink of Him, and rely on Him in our spirit.

BEING BAPTIZED IN THE SPIRIT AND DRINKING THE SPIRIT

Verse 3 of chapter 12 says, "Therefore I make known to you that no one speaking in the Spirit of God says, Jesus is accursed; and no one can say, Jesus is Lord! except in the Holy Spirit." Before the Spirit gives the spiritual gifts, He causes people to say, Jesus is Lord! Verse 4 continues, "But there are distinctions of gifts, but the same Spirit." Then verses 7 through 10 go on to speak of the manifestation of the Spirit given to each one for what is profitable. Verses 11 and 12 say, "But the one and the same Spirit operates all these things, distributing to each one respectively even as He purposes. For even as the body is one and has many members, yet all the members of the body, being many, are one body, so also is the Christ." In the normal and proper sense, all the gifts and manifestations mentioned in these verses are something of Christ for the building up of the Body of Christ. Verse 12 tells us that the Body is even Christ Himself. We should not isolate the gifts from Christ. They are something of Christ and for the Body of Christ.

Verse 13 continues, "For also in one Spirit we were all baptized into one Body, whether Jews or Greeks, whether slaves or free, and were all given to drink one Spirit." To be baptized in the Spirit and to drink the Spirit are two different matters. To be baptized in water is to be put into the water, but to drink the water is to take the water into us. We need the baptism of the Holy Spirit without, and we also need to drink the Spirit within. We are not baptized in water every day, but we drink water every day. In the same way, we need to drink the Spirit inwardly every day.

CHRIST BEING THE LIFE-GIVING SPIRIT

Finally, 15:45b says, "The last Adam became a life-giving Spirit." The last Adam is Christ. First Corinthians, a book that presents Christ to us as our portion, concludes by telling us that this Christ, who is our portion given by God, is the life-giving Spirit.

CHAPTER FIVE

THE TRANSFORMING SPIRIT
IN 2 CORINTHIANS

Scripture Reading: 2 Cor. 1:21-22; 3:3, 6, 8, 17, 18; 4:7, 16; 5:5; 12:8-9; 13:14

In the book of Romans, the Spirit is the Spirit of life, the Spirit of Christ, and the Spirit of the Son of God for our sonship to make us the real sons of God so that Christ may be the Firstborn among many brothers. These many sons of God and brothers of Christ are the living members that form the Body of Christ as His corporate expression. Then in 1 Corinthians, the Spirit is the indwelling Spirit who reveals to us all the things of Christ to bring us into the enjoyment, the fellowship, of all His riches, and through this enjoyment He builds us up together as one Body. Thus, He is the building Spirit. As the Spirit for our sonship in Romans, He is the Spirit of life, and as the building Spirit in 1 Corinthians, He is the indwelling and revealing Spirit. This is the message of Romans and 1 Corinthians concerning the Spirit.

In 2 Corinthians, the Spirit is the transforming Spirit (3:18). For the building up of God's house there is the need of transformation. This means that we all must be metabolically and inwardly changed in life, nature, and disposition and be renewed in our mind, will, and emotion. In this way we are wholly transformed in our soul. Then we will be the precious materials that are good for the building up of God's habitation.

The thought of transformation is also found in Romans. Romans 12:2 says, "Be transformed by the renewing of the mind." We are transformed in our soul by the renewing of the mind, emotion, and will. In 1 Corinthians 3 there is the thought of transformation, although this specific word is not in this Epistle. This chapter tells us that we must build the temple of God with gold, silver, and precious stones, rather than with wood, grass, and stubble (vv. 12, 16). Along with the building Spirit in 1 Corinthians there is the thought of the need of transformation for the building. Now the following book, 2 Corinthians, tells us that this indwelling, building Spirit is the Spirit who transforms us. Therefore, we may state in a simple way that in Romans He is the Spirit of the Son for our sonship, in 1 Corinthians He is the building Spirit, and in 2 Corinthians He is the transforming Spirit.

THE ANOINTING SPIRIT

Second Corinthians 1:21 and 22 say, "The One who firmly attaches us with you unto Christ and has anointed us is God, He who has also sealed us and given the Spirit in our hearts as a pledge." We should highlight the words *anointed, sealed,* and *pledge*. These are precious words. *Pledge* is equal to the modern terms *guarantee, security deposit*, or *down payment*. A down payment is the first payment and a guarantee of future payments. The Holy Spirit given to us by God today is the down payment, deposit, and guarantee of a future payment. Ephesians 1:13-14 also tells us that God has sealed us with the Holy Spirit and given us the Spirit as the pledge of our inheritance. In addition to sealing and pledging, 2 Corinthians 1 speaks of a third item, the anointing. God has anointed us with the Spirit, sealed us by and with the Spirit, and given us the Spirit as a pledge.

According to the sequence in verses 21 and 22, the anointing is first, followed by the sealing and the pledge. In typology, the oil of the anointing ointment signifies the Spirit. We may compare the ointment to paint. In this sense, to anoint is to paint. The more we paint something, the more the paint is added to that thing. Originally, it may have been only wood with a natural color, but as we paint it, the paint is added to the wood and even worked into it. God Himself is the anointing ointment, the "paint." For God to anoint us means that He paints us with Himself, and the more He anoints us, the more His element is added to us and wrought into us. Moreover, the ingredients of this anointing are all the elements of God. Thus, as He anoints us with Himself, His "ingredients" are being worked into us; that is, we have more of His element within us.

After a certain amount of painting, the paint and the thing that is painted are mingled as one. Likewise, God is within us in Christ as the Spirit of God and the Spirit of Christ to anoint us. It is by this anointing that God works Himself into us and mingles Himself with us. God has anointed us and is still anointing us with Himself, that is, with His Spirit as the ointment, so that we may have His elements, His ingredients. This must be very clear to us; it is vital to the Christian life.

THE SEALING SPIRIT

Second, verse 22 says that God has sealed us. According to the custom of the ancient times, for someone to seal something meant that he put a mark, a likeness, on that thing to signify that it belonged to him. Likewise, for God to seal us means that He puts His likeness upon us as a mark. The more God seals us, the more we have God-likeness as a mark that we belong to Him. On a certain occasion I went to a ship pier to meet a new believer. I had only received a cable concerning him, but I had never seen him, even in a photograph. As hundreds of people come off a ship, it is usually difficult to recognize anyone. However, this did not bother me. While people flooded out of the ship, I simply kept watching until I saw a person upon whom God had placed His mark. Then I knew that this one must be a brother. There was no outward mark upon him, simply a certain kind of expression by which I could recognize him as a brother.

Once in 1933 a sister sent us a letter telling us that she was coming to us from Shanghai. Again, we had never seen her, but we went to wait for her. As the ship stood at a distance, a number of small sampans carried people to the shore. With so many small boats in the sea, it is was difficult to find a particular person. However, as we were watching from the pier, I told the brothers, "Look, there is one person in the third boat. I believe she must be the sister." All the other brothers agreed that she must be the one, and indeed it was she. There is a certain kind of seal, a mark, placed upon us through the work of the Spirit. From our appearance, our countenance, people can recognize that we are children of God, those who belong to the Lord. This is a living mark as the outer operation of the inner Spirit. When we have the Holy Spirit within us, God causes us by the Spirit to have His likeness. This does not mean that we merely behave in a certain way. Even if we do nothing but stand here, the believers can still recognize that we are children of God, their brothers and sisters. This is because of the sealing of the Holy Spirit.

As we are being anointed by God with the Spirit, spontaneously we have this mark. In a sense, the anointing itself is the sealing. People often use paint to mark certain items. If we paint something in this way, this means it belongs to us. The anointing is the marking. It is a shame if others cannot tell whether we are children of God or children of the devil (1 John 3:10). We need to have a living mark, a living seal, that tells others that we belong to God, that we are children of God. We should have a certain kind of likeness that is the mark of God. God has marked us, sealed us, with the anointing Spirit. However, it is sometimes not easy to recognize whether or not someone is a brother. This is because the "paint" is not deep and rich enough in him. If the mark upon us is not clear, this means that we are short of God's anointing.

THE PLEDGING SPIRIT

Third, verse 22 speaks of the pledge. The pledge is the proof, guarantee, and down payment that all that God is, is our portion. The seal means that we belong to God, and the pledge guarantees that God belongs to us. The seal declares that we are God's, and the pledge declares that God is ours. God has given us the Holy Spirit within as a down payment of our future enjoyment. The Holy Spirit within us today is the firstfruit and foretaste of our enjoyment of Him, guaranteeing that God will give us the full enjoyment. God has anointed His ingredients into us, and He has sealed us with Himself as a mark. In addition, He has put the Holy Spirit within us as a down payment, a guarantee, and a deposit to ensure that all that God is, is our portion. This is the work of the Holy Spirit within us. The anointing, the sealing, and the pledging are all for the purpose of transforming us. The more God anoints us, the more He seals us, and the more we enjoy the pledging Spirit, the more we are transformed.

THE INSCRIBING SPIRIT
TO WRITE LIVING LETTERS OF CHRIST

Chapter 3 reveals the Spirit in five aspects. First, verse 3 says, "Since you are being manifested that you are a letter of Christ ministered by us, inscribed not with ink but with the Spirit of the living God; not in tablets of stone but in tablets of hearts of flesh." The Spirit here is the writing Spirit to write Christ into us, and our heart is the tablet for the inscribing Spirit. We are the living letters, and the "story" written on these letters is Christ. Moreover, the writer of these letters is the Spirit through the apostles, and the ink also is the Spirit. The indwelling Spirit is continually writing something of Christ upon our heart.

Christ today has come into our spirit, but He may not yet be written on our heart. Our heart mainly surrounds our spirit, being composed of our mind, emotion, and will, in addition to our conscience. Therefore, for the Spirit to write Christ on us as living letters means that He writes Christ into our mind, emotion, and will; that is, the Spirit takes our whole heart as the tablet for inscribing Christ. As He does this, we become a complete epistle of Christ, and people can read Christ upon us. When people "read" our mind, emotion, and will, they will say, "Every bit of this person is Christ. His thought is Christ, his love is Christ, and even his hating is Christ (Rev. 2:6). Moreover, his deciding is also Christ. His deciding to keep something is Christ, and his deciding to reject it also is Christ." I am afraid that sometimes people cannot read Christ upon our mind, emotion, and will. When they read our heart, they may read only our car or our bank account. What is written on our mind, emotion, will? Has Christ been written on, that is, wrought into, our heart?

To inscribe Christ in our heart is the work of the transforming Spirit within us. The transforming Spirit is waiting for the opportunity to write Christ into our mind, emotion, and will to make us complete epistles of Christ. The indwelling Spirit, who is the transforming Spirit, is doing the work of writing in us, but we need to give Him our cooperation. We must let Him have the free course to write something into our mind, emotion, and will.

THE MINISTERING SPIRIT

Verse 6a goes on to say, "Who has also made us sufficient as ministers of a new covenant, ministers not of the letter but of the Spirit." As ministers of the word today, we must be the good writers of Christ into others. This means that we must minister Christ to people to cause those who listen to our message to become the living epistles of Christ. *Ministers not of the letter but of the Spirit* indicates that the Spirit here is the ministering Spirit to minister, to write, Christ into us. Verse 8 also speaks of "the ministry of the Spirit."

THE LIFE-GIVING SPIRIT

Verse 6b continues, "For the letter kills, but the Spirit gives life." Here the Spirit is the life-giving Spirit to always impart life into us. Life includes satisfaction; to be satisfied means that we are full of life. Life also includes strength; to be weak means that we are short of life, but to be full of strength means we are full of life. In addition, to be in the light and full of light means that we are full of life, but to be in darkness means that we are short of life. When we have rest, comfort, and peace, that also means that we have life, but to be short of these indicates that we are short of life. The life-giving Spirit always ministers life and the life supply to us.

THE LIBERATING SPIRIT

Verse 17 says, "And the Lord is the Spirit; and where the Spirit of the Lord is, there is freedom." *The Spirit* in verse 17 refers to the Spirit who gives life in verse 6. In verse 17 the Spirit is the liberating Spirit, liberating us from every kind of bondage, particularly from the bondage and veiling of the law. By the work of this liberating Spirit we are released from any kind of covering and bondage. We have been liberated. However, we still need to give Him the ground, the opportunity, and the free course to do His liberating work. This verse says, "Where the Spirit of the Lord is, there is freedom." This means that He must be with us and He must have the ground in us. If He is not with us, we do not have freedom; if He does not gain the ground in us, we cannot obtain freedom. On the other hand, if the ground in us is His, the freedom is ours. He is the liberating Spirit, liberating us from every kind of bondage, suppression, oppression, and occupation, but we must give Him the ground in us.

THE TRANSFORMING SPIRIT

Verse 18 says, "But we all with unveiled face, beholding and reflecting like a mirror the glory of the Lord, are being transformed into the same image from glory to glory, even as from the Lord Spirit." We are mirrors that reflect while we behold. However, we must have an unveiled face. If our face is veiled and covered, the mirror will not function. As we behold the Lord, we reflect His glory, and by this beholding and reflecting, we are gradually transformed to the image of the Lord from glory to glory. This transformation is the work of the transforming Spirit. In chapters 1 and 3 there are eight items related to the Spirit: anointing, sealing, pledging, inscribing, ministering, life-giving, liberating, and transforming. The first seven aspects are all for the purpose of transformation. The Spirit within us continually anoints us, seals us, and gives us the assurance that God is ours. He also inscribes Christ into us, ministers Christ to us, imparts life to us, and liberates us from bondage. All this is so that He can transform us into the image of Christ.

I would ask you all, especially the young brothers and sisters, to memorize all these items: anointing, sealing, pledging, inscribing, ministering, life-giving, liberating, and transforming. What we must always do is open ourselves to Him, not only from our heart but also from our spirit. We must open ourselves from the depths of our being so that we may truly have an unveiled face, a face with no covering or hindrance. If we are open to Him, the transforming Spirit will be free to work within us to transform us into the glorious image of Christ from glory to glory.

CHRIST AS THE TREASURE
IN OUR REGENERATED SPIRIT
AND THE RENEWING OF THE INNER MAN

Verse 7 of chapter 4 says, "We have this treasure in earthen vessels that the excellency of the power may be of God and not out of us." Then verse 16 says, "Therefore we do not lose heart; but though our outer man is decaying, yet our inner man is being renewed day by day." The outer man is the old soul with the body as its organ to express it, and the inner man is our regenerated human spirit with our renewed soul as its organ to express it. This implies that the life of the soul must be "whittled down," crossed out, but the function of the soul must be renewed so that the soul as an organ can be used by the regenerated spirit.

The treasure in verse 7 is Christ in our regenerated spirit. Now we need to cooperate with the indwelling Spirit to live no longer by the soul but always by the spirit. The outer man must be crossed out so that we can give the Spirit the opportunity to renew our inner man day by day. This renewing of the inner man is mainly not in the spirit but in the soul—the mind, emotion, and will. Our spirit has been renewed and regenerated already, but now our soul must be renewed. Therefore, we must always cooperate with the indwelling Spirit so that He may spread Christ as the treasure from our spirit into our soul for the renewing of the soul day by day.

THE SPIRIT AS THE PLEDGE
OF OUR HEAVENLY TABERNACLE

Verse 5 of chapter 5 says, "Now He who has wrought us for this very thing is God, who has given to us the Spirit as a pledge." Again we have the Spirit as the guarantee, the pledge, but here the guarantee is for a heavenly tabernacle, a glorious body (vv. 1-2). At the present time we are in a temporary, earthen body, but the Lord promises us that one day He will change our body into a glorious one. The guarantee and foretaste of this is the Spirit. The apostle Paul was not waiting to die; rather, he was expecting to have a change from his temporary tabernacle to an eternal, permanent one, which is a glorious body. Because our body is very weak, it is a real bothering to us. By the Spirit, however, even this weak body is enlivened and strengthened. This is a foretaste of the change awaiting our body.

CHRIST AS SUFFICIENT GRACE IN OUR HUMAN SPIRIT

In 12:8 and 9, Paul says about the thorn in his flesh, "Concerning this I entreated the Lord three times that it might depart from me. And He has said to me, My grace is sufficient for you, for My power is perfected in weakness. Most gladly therefore I will rather boast in my weaknesses that the power of Christ might tabernacle over me." The Lord would not take away the thorn. Rather, He supplied Paul with sufficient grace for his suffering. Grace is the Lord's power, and this power is the Lord Himself. The Lord Himself as the power to us is the grace we enjoy.

The Lord's sufficient grace is in our spirit. Galatians 6:18 says, "The grace of our Lord Jesus Christ be with your spirit, brothers. Amen." Philemon 25 says, "The grace of the Lord Jesus Christ be with your spirit." Regrettably, many Christians know, "My grace is sufficient," but very few know that this sufficient grace is in our spirit. In order to enjoy, apply, and appropriate this sufficient grace, we need to know that it is in our spirit, and we need to know how to exercise our spirit.

Some may say that since Paul's suffering in 2 Corinthians 12 was in his body, the grace must also be in the body. This is not the case. Grace is in our spirit. When our spirit is strong, we can endure any kind of suffering in the body, but when our spirit is weak, the suffering of the body becomes a suffering to our whole being. Even if there is a certain amount of suffering in our body, our whole being will not suffer if our spirit within is strong. We are strengthened and we can endure any suffering because we have grace in our spirit.

THE FELLOWSHIP OF THE HOLY SPIRIT TRANSMITTING INTO US THE GRACE OF CHRIST WITH THE LOVE OF GOD

Verse 14 of chapter 13 concludes, "The grace of the Lord Jesus Christ and the love of God and the fellowship of the Holy Spirit be with you all." In this verse we have the Triune

God—the Father, the Son, and the Spirit. God is in Christ, and Christ is the Spirit. God as the source is love, Christ as the course is grace, and the Spirit as the flow is fellowship. Second Corinthians shows us how to enjoy Christ as our sufficient grace. The source of this grace is the love of God, and the course of this love is grace. In other words, love is the source, and grace is the expression of the source. This grace comes into us by the flow, the fellowship, the transmission, of the Spirit.

Love, grace, and fellowship are simply the Triune God Himself. Love is God, and this love, who is God Himself, is the source. Out of this love, Christ comes as our grace, and Christ as grace comes into us by the transmission of the Holy Spirit. Christians often use this verse as a benediction, but it is regrettable that many do not know what it means. This verse reveals the work of the transforming Spirit to transmit into us Christ as the grace from God Himself as love, the source. Out of God Himself as love, the transforming Spirit continually transmits and communicates Christ into us as our sufficient grace. Now we simply enjoy and experience this grace, and it is in this grace that day by day we are being transformed into His image. The process of this transforming work is being carried out by the fellowship of the Holy Spirit. Therefore, at the conclusion of this book Paul commends to us the grace of the Lord Jesus Christ, the love of God, and the fellowship of the Holy Spirit so that we may be transformed.

CHAPTER SIX

THE PROMISED SPIRIT
AS THE BLESSING OF THE GOSPEL
IN GALATIANS

Scripture Reading: Gal. 1:16a; 2:20; 3:27; 4:19; 3:2-3, 5, 8, 13-14; 4:4-6, 29; 5:16-18, 22-23, 25; 6:1, 8, 18

The verses in Galatians listed in the Scripture reading above unveil the experience of Christ in four aspects. First, 1:16a says, "To reveal His Son in me." Then 2:20 says, "It is Christ who lives in me." Verse 19 of chapter 4 says, "Christ is formed in you." Then 3:27 says, "For as many of you as were baptized into Christ have put on Christ." After being revealed in us, Christ is now living in us, and He is being formed in us. Moreover, we are clothed with Christ. Christ is our inner life and content, and He is also our outer expression. He is in us as our life, and we are in Him as our expression. In this way we are one with Him.

How can Christ be revealed in us, live in us, and be formed in us, and how can we put Him on? It is only by the Spirit. Apart from the Spirit it is not possible to experience Christ in this way. In addition to showing us that God's intention, desire, and pleasure are to reveal Christ in us, have Christ living in us, have Christ formed in us, and clothe us with Christ, the book of Galatians speaks much concerning the Spirit. The Spirit in this book has a specific position, because without the Spirit it is not possible for us to experience Christ.

THE PROMISED SPIRIT
AS THE BLESSING OF THE GOSPEL

Verse 8 of chapter 3 says, "The Scripture, foreseeing that God would justify the Gentiles out of faith, announced the gospel beforehand to Abraham: 'In you shall all the nations be blessed.'" We may consider that the gospel began to be preached at the earliest by John the Baptist. However, this verse tells us that the gospel was preached to Abraham in Genesis 12. The key to understanding Galatians 3 is to know what the blessing is that God announced to Abraham. Verses 13 and 14 say, "Christ has redeemed us out of the curse of the law, having become a curse on our behalf; because it is written, 'Cursed is everyone hanging on a tree'; in order that the blessing of Abraham might come to the Gentiles in Christ Jesus, that we might receive the promise of the Spirit through faith." To receive the promise of the Spirit is to receive the Spirit who was promised. Therefore, the blessing that God promised to Abraham is the Spirit, who would be given to the nations in Christ.

These two verses speak of two matters. On the negative side, Christ has redeemed us, and on the positive side, the purpose of redemption is that we may have the Spirit whom God promised. John 1:29 says, "Behold, the Lamb of God, who takes away the sin of the world!" Then verse 32 adds, "John testified, saying, I beheld the Spirit descending as a dove out of heaven, and He abode upon Him." Here we have the Lamb and the dove. The Lamb is for redemption, and the dove is the Spirit. On the negative side, the Lamb redeems us to bring us back to God, and on the positive side, the Spirit fulfills God's eternal purpose. The blessing that God promised to Abraham is that He would give the Spirit to the nations through Christ as the seed of Abraham.

In John 1, the dove descended upon the Lamb. The Lamb signifies redemption, and the dove signifies the life-giving Spirit. This indicates that the life-giving Spirit comes to us on the basis of the redemption of Christ. Since God is Triune, when we consider who the Spirit is, we must trace Him back to Christ. Then when we ask who Christ is, we must trace Him back to God. God is the fullness, Christ is the embodiment and expression of the fullness of God (Col. 2:9), and the Spirit is the reality of all that Christ is (John 14:17). Stated another way, God the Father is the source, God the Son is the expression, and God the Spirit is the transmission (2 Cor.

13:14). Therefore, the Spirit is the reality of the Triune God; that is, He is the reality of all that the Triune God is, all that He has accomplished, and all that He has obtained and attained. The central item and blessing of the gospel preached to Abraham was that God would give this Spirit to all the chosen ones.

In this Spirit is God the Father, God the Son, the divine nature, the human nature, and Christ's incarnation, human living, crucifixion for redemption, resurrection with the power of life, glorification, ascension, enthronement, headship, lordship, kingship, and transcendence. All these are realized in the all-inclusive Spirit. God promised Abraham that He would give such a blessing to all the nations through faith. The nations who believe in Christ as the unique seed of Abraham are blessed by this Spirit. If we realize the Spirit in this way, Galatians 3 will be open to us.

THE SPIRIT BEING BOUNTIFULLY SUPPLIED TO US

Galatians 3:2 and 3 say, "This only I wish to learn from you, Did you receive the Spirit out of the works of law or out of the hearing of faith? Are you so foolish? Having begun by the Spirit, are you now being perfected by the flesh?" Verse 5 continues, "He therefore who bountifully supplies to you the Spirit and does works of power among you, does He do it out of the works of law or out of the hearing of faith?" *Bountifully supplies* is one word in the Greek text; it is the verb form of the noun in Philippians 1:19, which speaks of "the bountiful supply of the Spirit of Jesus Christ." God not only gives us the Spirit but supplies the Spirit to us bountifully. There is a difference between giving and supplying. To give may be only once for all, but to supply is to give continually. Like a power plant that constantly supplies electricity, God continually supplies the Spirit to us. At the time of Abraham, God promised the Spirit described in Galatians 3. Then after Christ came and accomplished redemption, this promised Spirit was given to us and is now being supplied to us. We have received this Spirit, and now having begun in the Spirit, we need to go on to be perfected in Him.

THE SPIRIT OF THE SON OF GOD
BEING SENT INTO OUR HEARTS FOR OUR SONSHIP

Galatians 4:4-5 says, "When the fullness of the time came, God sent forth His Son, born of a woman, born under law, that He might redeem those under law that we might receive the sonship." Verse 5 does not say that God sent forth His Son to redeem us so that we may go to heaven. This is the incorrect gospel that many Christians preach. Rather, Christ redeemed us that we might receive the sonship. Verse 6 continues, "And because you are sons, God has sent forth the Spirit of His Son into our hearts, crying, Abba, Father!" The way we know that the Spirit of the Son of God has been sent into us is that there is a cry within us. For us to cry, "Abba, Father!" is a proof that we have the Spirit of the Son of God. Before we believed in Christ, we could not cry, "Abba, Father." However, after we believed in Jesus, there was immediately a desire within us to cry to God in this way. Now the more we cry in this way, the more we have the sweetness within. This proves that the Spirit of the Son of God has been sent into us. After our new birth by the Spirit, the Spirit of the Son of God is within us.

Someone may wonder whether or not he has the Spirit of the Son of God within him. Once a classmate of Brother Watchman Nee asked him, "How can I know that I am a child of God and that I have the Spirit of the Son of God?" Brother Nee replied, "I know that you are married. The first time you saw your father-in-law, were you able to call him 'Father' with a sense of sweetness?" The classmate answered that he was reluctant to address him in such a manner. Brother Nee asked, "Have you ever called your own father 'Father' in a reluctant way?" The classmate replied that it was always with gladness that he called his father "Father." The reason he could not call his father-in-law "Father" was that this man was not his actual father. God is our Father, not our "Father-in-law." We do not call him Father reluctantly but willingly and with much gladness. Especially when we face troubles and hardships, we come to God, crying, "O Father! Abba, Father." The more we call Him in this way, the more comfort and sweetness we sense within. This is a strong proof that we have received the Spirit of the Son of God within us. We are born of the Spirit, and the Spirit of the Son has come into us crying, "Abba, Father." Now this all-inclusive, wonderful, marvelous, and rich Spirit is within us.

BORN ACCORDING TO THE SPIRIT

Verse 29 says, "Just as at that time he who was born according to the flesh persecuted him who was born according to the Spirit, so also it is now." This verse speaks of our birth by the Spirit. When the Spirit came to us, we received Him in the way of birth; that is, He came into us to regenerate us.

THE FRUIT OF THE SPIRIT
BEING CHRIST EXPRESSED IN US
THROUGH OUR WALKING BY THE SPIRIT

Verses 22 and 23 of chapter 5 say, "The fruit of the Spirit is love, joy, peace, long-suffering, kindness, goodness, faithfulness, meekness, self-control; against such things there is no law." All of these items are not different kinds of fruit. Rather, verse 22 speaks of "the fruit," singular in number. The fruit is one, but the aspects of this fruit are many. The one fruit is Christ expressed through us by the Spirit. These verses list nine items, but there are many more than nine aspects of the one fruit. Lowliness, humility, tenderness, purity, godliness, and holiness are all not listed here. This proves that these nine items are not all-inclusive. They are simply examples of the aspects of the fruit of the Spirit, which is Christ expressed in us.

Verses 16 through 18 say, "But I say, Walk by the Spirit and you shall by no means fulfill the lust of the flesh. For the flesh lusts against the Spirit, and the Spirit against the flesh; for these oppose each other that you would not do the things that you desire. But if you are led by the Spirit, you are not under the law." Verse 25 continues, "If we live by the Spirit, let us also walk by the Spirit." After being born of the Spirit, and after the Spirit has come into us, we simply need to walk in Him. To walk includes many matters. All that we do and speak and even our entire being must be in this Spirit. As we have life in this Spirit, so we must also walk in Him.

The Spirit has regenerated us, and He is now dwelling in our spirit. Therefore, we simply need to learn one thing, that is, to constantly walk in Him and do everything in Him. Then spontaneously we will bear fruit. To bear fruit is not a work carried out by a branch. Rather, it is the outworking of the inner life within the branch. When we walk in the Spirit, live in the Spirit, and sow unto the Spirit, this indwelling Spirit produces fruit. This fruit is the outworking of the inner Spirit in many aspects as the expression of Christ.

RESTORING A BROTHER IN A SPIRIT OF MEEKNESS

Verse 1 of chapter 6 says, "Brothers, even if a man is overtaken in some offense, you who are spiritual restore such a one in a spirit of meekness, looking to yourself lest you also be tempted." Even when we do the good work of restoring a fallen brother, we must do it not in our self or soul but in our spirit. Then we will be a spiritual person. All of the verses mentioned above prove that after we are born again in our spirit and the Holy Spirit comes into us, we must walk, live, and do everything in the spirit.

SOWING UNTO THE SPIRIT

Verse 8 says, "For he who sows unto his own flesh will reap corruption of the flesh, but he who sows unto the Spirit will of the Spirit reap eternal life." We must not only walk in the Spirit but also sow unto the Spirit. Then we will have something of the Spirit to reap as a harvest.

THE GRACE OF OUR LORD JESUS CHRIST BEING WITH OUR SPIRIT

The last verse of Galatians says, "The grace of our Lord Jesus Christ be with your spirit, brothers. Amen" (6:18). This verse does not say that the grace of the Lord is with our mind, heart, soul, or body. Rather, the grace of the Lord is with our spirit. This grace is Christ Himself transmitted into us as the Spirit. Therefore, the Spirit is the grace, and this grace is in our spirit. Now we simply need to set our mind on the spirit (Rom. 8:6), come back to our spirit to touch and enjoy the grace, and exercise our spirit to contact the Lord. When we do this, we will immediately realize that the Lord is within us as the grace for our need.

THE CENTRAL MESSAGE OF THE BOOK OF GALATIANS

Because the order of the books of the New Testament was arranged by the Holy Spirit, the sequence of the Epistles is very meaningful. In Romans we have the Spirit of the Son of God for our sonship, making us the sons of God so that Christ can be the Firstborn among many brothers. Then in 1 Corinthians there is the building Spirit to give us the growth in life and build us together as the house, the temple of God. In 2 Corinthians we have the transforming Spirit, because for God's building there is the need for transformation. The Spirit who builds us together as the house of God also transforms us. Following this, Galatians tells us that we are one with Christ and that He is one with us. Christ is revealed in us, lives in us, and is formed within us, and we put Him on to be clothed with Him. All this is by the Spirit, who is the blessing promised by God to Abraham. When God called Abraham, He preached the gospel to him, promising him that this blessing would be given not only to him and to his descendants but also to all the nations who would believe in the one seed. Through and based upon the redemption that Christ accomplished, the Spirit that was promised to Abraham came as the all-inclusive wonderful One with many items. He first came into our deadened spirit to make it alive, to regenerate us in the spirit. Then He remains in our spirit as the Spirit of the Son of God.

On the negative side, the message of the book of Galatians is that we should not care for the law, that is, for trying to do good. We should not try to love our wife in our self. The more we try to love our wife, the more we may be a terrible husband. We need to forget about trying to keep the law in this way. Rather, each of us should say, "I am dead to the law, even to the law of loving my wife in my self." Likewise, the sisters should not consider that they need to submit to their husband in their self. Submitting to their husband must not be a law. By her flesh, a sister may be able to submit to her husband today, but tomorrow she may no longer be able. Instead, the sisters should be dead to the law of submitting. We should not care for doing good in our self. We must realize that our flesh is good for nothing but to be put on the cross. We should not try to do good or overcome by our self. We can never overcome by exercising our flesh to accomplish something.

On the positive side, we need to realize that God's intention, desire, and pleasure are to reveal Christ in us, for Christ to live in us, be formed in us, and be wrought into us as our everything, and for us to be clothed with Christ. This is a matter of dealing not with good but with Christ. For this purpose, we must also realize that the Spirit of the Son of God is now in us. He has been given to us and is now being supplied to us. Therefore, we need not to do good but simply to walk in the Spirit, have our being in the Spirit, sow unto the Spirit, and work in the Spirit. Then there will be the outworking of the expression of Christ, which is the fruit of the Spirit in many aspects, including love, peace, joy, and many items.

The book of Galatians reveals not the demand of the law but the grace in our spirit. This grace is simply Christ as the Spirit for our enjoyment. We must learn to turn back to the Spirit to touch this grace. If we open to this grace, it will become living water, flowing within us for our enjoyment and nourishment. Then everything will come out of this flow. This salvation of God in Christ through the Spirit is the central message of the book of Galatians.

In Galatians, the law is versus Christ, and the flesh is versus the Spirit. The law is always related to the flesh, and Christ is related to our spirit. To try to keep the law is to exercise the flesh, but to live by Christ and live out Christ requires us to exercise our spirit. The cross has dealt with the flesh, and the law of the commandments in ordinances has been crucified (Eph. 2:15). By dealing with all negative matters, the cross prepared the way for the Spirit. Now when we are in our spirit, we touch Christ, enjoy Christ, and experience Christ, and Christ becomes our grace.

There are five main items in Galatians: the law, the flesh, Christ, the Spirit, and the cross. The flesh, including the law, has been dealt with on the cross. Now we have Christ as the Spirit. Therefore, we need to walk by the Spirit, live in the

Spirit, sow unto the Spirit, and do everything in the Spirit for God's pleasure. When we are in our spirit, we are one with Christ, and Christ becomes grace to us for our enjoyment and our fruit as His expression through the outworking of the inner Spirit. This is the way of God's salvation.

CHAPTER SEVEN

THE WORK OF THE SPIRIT IN EPHESIANS

Scripture Reading: Eph. 1:3, 13-14, 17-23; 3:3-5; 2:18, 22; 3:16-17a; 4:3-4, 23; 5:18; 6:17-18

The two main subjects of the New Testament—Christ as life and the church as Christ's expression—can be seen in the two books of Galatians and Ephesians. Galatians tells us that Christ is our life, and in Ephesians we see the church as the Body of Christ. In Galatians the Spirit is for us to take Christ as our life, live by Christ, and live out Christ. Then in Ephesians the Spirit is for us, as the members of Christ, to realize and experience the Body.

PARTAKING OF THE BLESSINGS OF THE HOLY SPIRIT IN OUR HUMAN SPIRIT

In this message we will consider ten points concerning the Spirit in Ephesians. As the introduction to the book of Ephesians, 1:3 says, "Blessed be the God and Father of our Lord Jesus Christ, who has blessed us with every spiritual blessing in the heavenlies in Christ." Everything from this verse to the end of the book may be considered as items of the spiritual blessings. The blessings with which God has blessed the church as the Body of Christ are spiritual blessings. Therefore, they are in the Holy Spirit and must be realized by us in our human spirit. If these blessings were physical, material blessings, they would need to be enjoyed and experienced by us in our physical body. Likewise, if they were psychological blessings, we could realize them by exercising our soul—our mind, emotion, and will. However, these are spiritual blessings, the blessings of the Holy Spirit. Since the nature of all these blessings is spiritual, we need to exercise our spirit to realize, enjoy, and partake of them in our spirit.

In certain verses in Ephesians, it is difficult for translators of the Bible to discern whether the word *spirit* refers to the Holy Spirit or to our human spirit. In actuality, all the blessings mentioned in this book are spiritual blessings of the Holy Spirit, which we can realize only in our spirit. This is the principle set forth in John 4:24, which says, "God is Spirit, and those who worship Him must worship in spirit and truthfulness."

THE HOLY SPIRIT AS THE SEAL AND THE PLEDGE

Ephesians 1:13 says, "In whom you also, having heard the word of the truth, the gospel of your salvation, in Him also believing, you were sealed with the Holy Spirit of the promise." We should not question whether or not we have the Holy Spirit as a seal within us, but whether we have believed in Christ. To believe is our responsibility, and to seal is His. At the same time we believed in Christ, we were sealed with the Holy Spirit. To seal something is to put a mark on it. For us to be sealed is to have the Spirit Himself within us as a divine mark. God has put the Holy Spirit into us as a divine mark to prove, testify, and declare that we are His inheritance. How can we know that we are God's inheritance? It is because the Bible tells us that God has confirmed our believing in Him by sealing us with His Spirit. Also, the sealing Spirit Himself deep within confirms that we have been marked out and gives us the likeness and appearance of God (2 Cor. 1:21-22). This divine appearance and likeness is the mark, the seal, that confirms that we belong to God as His children and His inheritance.

Ephesians 1:14 continues, "Who is the pledge of our inheritance unto the redemption of the acquired possession, to the praise of His glory." The Holy Spirit within us is the pledge, earnest, down payment, deposit, guarantee, foretaste, firstfruit, and sample. A salesman often offers people a sample of his product. In the same way, the Holy Spirit within us is the sample, the foretaste, of our enjoyment of God. This sample is the down payment, deposit, pledge, and earnest to guarantee that God is our portion. The Holy Spirit is the seal and the pledge for a two-way traffic. The seal testifies that we are God's inheritance, and the pledge proves that God is our portion and enjoyment.

THE REVEALING SPIRIT IN OUR SPIRIT

From this point, the book of Ephesians goes on to reveal eight aspects of the Holy Spirit's work within us. These are further spiritual blessings of the Spirit that are realized in our spirit. The Spirit first works as the revealing Spirit to reveal to us the spiritual blessings. Verses 17 and 18 say, "That the God of our Lord Jesus Christ, the Father of glory, may give to you a spirit of wisdom and revelation in the full knowledge of Him, the eyes of your heart having been enlightened, that you may know what is the hope of His calling, and what are the riches of the glory of His inheritance in the saints." The spirit in verse 17 is our regenerated spirit indwelt by the Spirit of God. Verse 18 speaks of the eyes not of our body but of our heart. Therefore, to know actually means to see.

Being Enlightened to See the Eternal Things

Verses 19 through 23 continue, "And what is the surpassing greatness of His power toward us who believe, according to the operation of the might of His strength, which He caused to operate in Christ in raising Him from the dead and seating Him at His right hand in the heavenlies, far above all rule and authority and power and lordship and every name that is named not only in this age but also in that which is to come; and He subjected all things under His feet and gave Him to be Head over all things to the church, which is His Body, the fullness of the One who fills all in all." Have we ever thanked and praised the Lord for the fourfold power mentioned in these verses? Instead, we may have thanked the Lord for a good husband or wife, children, job, house, car, or college degree. We need to pray according to the prayer that the apostle Paul prayed in these verses, saying, "O Lord, I thank You not merely for the outward things but for the power toward us that operated in Christ to raise Him from the dead, seat Him at Your right hand in the heavenlies far above all, subject all things under His feet, and give Him to be Head over all things to the church." The reason we may not pray in this way is that we are blind to the eternal things. Behind our veil we may be able to see only a graduate degree, wife, husband, child, car, job, or house. We may not have seen the things beyond the veil. The veil must be taken away so that the eyes of our inner understanding may be enlightened to thoroughly see through to the eternal things in the heavenlies, including the hope of God's calling, the riches of the glory of God's inheritance in His saints, and the fourfold power that is toward us. When we see these matters, we will say, "Praise the Lord, Hallelujah!"

We need such a vision and revelation. No man can remove the veil from our eyes. Rather, we must look to the Lord that this veil will be riven and our eyes will be opened to see the glory, the hope, and the power mentioned in these verses. This is the work of the revealing Spirit. The Holy Spirit within us, who is the seal and the pledge, is now working to reveal, to unveil, all these things.

Having Understanding in the Mystery of Christ by a Revelation in Our Mingled Spirit

Ephesians 3:3-4 says, "By revelation the mystery was made known to me, as I have written previously in brief, by which, in reading it, you can perceive my understanding in the mystery of Christ." In Colossians 2:2 the mystery of God is Christ, who is the "story" of God, the explanation and expression of God. In Ephesians the mystery of Christ is the church, because the church is the "story" of Christ, His explanation and expression. Ephesians 3:5 continues, "Which in other generations was not made known to the sons of men, as it has now been revealed to His holy apostles and prophets in spirit." The spirit here is the human spirit of the apostles and prophets, a spirit regenerated and indwelt by the Holy Spirit of God. It can be considered the mingled spirit, the human spirit mingled with God's Spirit. To see the mystery of Christ, which is the Body of Christ, requires a revelation in our spirit by the Holy Spirit.

When we come to the book of Ephesians, we must not overly exercise our mentality to understand, analyze, or argue. Rather, we must learn to take the word of this book into our spirit. We should pray to bring whatever we read into our spirit and realize it in the spirit. In this way, we will receive not merely an understanding of the teachings but a revelation and a vision in our spirit. Such a vision is from the Holy Spirit in our human spirit. For example, 1:22b-23 says, "The church, which is His Body, the fullness of the One who fills all in all." We should not try to understand this merely with our mind. We need to take this word into our spirit by praying over it. We may say, "Lord, I praise You that the church is Your Body. This Body is Your fullness, and You are the One who fills all in all." If we pray in this way, we will receive this word into our spirit and realize it by our spirit. This will make a real difference. We will see that the church as the Body is the fullness of Christ. We will say, "Lord, I will sacrifice my whole life for Your Body." This is not an argument or an analyzing but a realization in the spirit. When the Spirit gives us a revelation, He also gives us the wisdom to grasp and understand what we see in this revelation. We need the revealing word of the indwelling Spirit, who is the seal and the earnest within our spirit. This is the first aspect of the work of the Spirit in Ephesians.

THE UNITING SPIRIT

The Holy Spirit also works to cause all those, to whom He reveals the things of the mystery of God and the mystery of Christ, to be one. Verse 18 of chapter 2 says, "For through Him we both have access in one Spirit unto the Father." *Both* refers to the Jewish and the Gentile believers. Formerly, the Jews were separated from the Gentiles, but now in the one Spirit the Jewish believers are one with the Gentile believers. They are made one not in doctrines, teachings, or forms but in one Spirit. Therefore, the Spirit who indwells all the believers is the Spirit of oneness.

If we merely study the teachings of the Bible, after a short time we may disagree with one another and be divided. However, the more we turn from merely studying to praying in the Spirit, the more we will have the uniting Spirit to be one. When we focus on mere teachings, we are divided, but when we are in the spirit, we are one. The Holy Spirit within us is the uniting Spirit, but we may not give Him the opportunity to make us one because we are exercising our mentality merely to know doctrinal teachings. The two peoples, the Jews and the Gentiles, were united as one by the one indwelling Spirit. Verse 3 of chapter 4 speaks of the oneness of the Spirit. The Spirit is the One who makes us one. First, He reveals the things of Christ to us, including the mystery of Christ, the church. Then He makes us one as His one Body.

THE BUILDING SPIRIT

The Spirit is also building us together. Verse 22 of chapter 2 says, "In whom you also are being built together into a dwelling place of God in spirit." The spirit here is the believers' human spirit, which is indwelt by God's Holy Spirit. The Holy Spirit works within us to reveal to us the things of God, to unite us together, and to build us up together as the habitation of God in spirit by mingling Himself with us. Verse 4 of chapter 4 speaks of "one Body and one Spirit." This indicates that the Spirit is the building Spirit for the Body, the Spirit that reveals, unites, and builds up the Body. The more we pay attention to doctrinal teachings, gifts, and outward power, the more we will be divided. However, if we would all turn from these things to the indwelling, sealing, and building Spirit, gradually and spontaneously we will be built up together.

THE STRENGTHENING SPIRIT

The Spirit within us is also the strengthening Spirit. Verse 16 of chapter 3 says, "That He would grant you, according to the riches of His glory, to be strengthened with power through His Spirit into the inner man." The two spirits—the indwelling Spirit and our human spirit, which is our inner man—are mingled together. However, if we do not give the Spirit the adequate ground in us, He is confined and restricted in our spirit. Therefore, our spirit may be weak. This is why we need the Holy Spirit to strengthen our regenerated spirit.

Verse 17 continues, "That Christ may make His home in

your hearts through faith." Our heart consists mainly of the soul, which is the part of our being surrounding our spirit. For Christ to make His home in our heart is for Him to spread into our soul. When the Holy Spirit strengthens our spirit, He gains more ground in us and has more opportunity to spread out of our spirit to saturate our heart. Then He is able to settle and make His home in our heart. The result, the issue, of the strengthening of the Spirit in our inner man is that we are filled unto all the fullness of God (v. 19).

THE RENEWING SPIRIT

The next aspect of the work of the Holy Spirit is that He renews all the parts of our soul—our mind, emotion, and will. Verse 23 of chapter 4 says, "And that you be renewed in the spirit of your mind." As our inner man is strengthened and the Spirit gains the opportunity to spread into all the parts of our soul, He becomes the renewing Spirit. *The spirit of your mind* is a particular term. Originally, the Spirit was only in our spirit, but after strengthening our spirit, He spreads into our mind, which is the leading part of the soul and of the heart. In this way our mingled spirit becomes the spirit of the mind. Originally, He is the Spirit only in our spirit, but now He becomes the renewing Spirit in our mind. We can prove this by our experience. When we give Him the ground, the opportunity, to spread into all the parts of our being, we experience the renewing of the Spirit in our mind, emotion, and will.

THE FILLING SPIRIT

Verse 18 of chapter 5 says, "Do not be drunk with wine, in which is dissoluteness, but be filled in spirit." To be drunk is to be filled in the body with wine, but to be filled in spirit is to be filled in our human spirit with the Holy Spirit. We are not persons who are filled with wine; we are persons who are full of the Holy Spirit in our spirit. This divine, spiritual, and heavenly wine is the Spirit, who is God Himself. We need to drink of Him all day long. We are drinkers of the Spirit who are filled with the Holy Spirit in our spirit. The Holy Spirit is the filling Spirit, the Spirit who is working to strengthen, renew, and fill us within.

THE SLAYING SPIRIT

After we have been strengthened, renewed, and filled within, we are equipped and qualified to do the work of fighting as an army. We see this aspect in chapter 6. Verse 17 says, "Receive the helmet of salvation and the sword of the Spirit, which Spirit is the word of God." The Spirit here is the slaying Spirit as the sword of God to kill the enemy. All the foregoing items are in a proper sequence. Ephesians begins with the revealing Spirit, followed by the uniting, building up, strengthening, renewing, and filling Spirit. After experiencing the Spirit in all these ways, we are qualified to know Him as the slaying Spirit.

THE PRAYING SPIRIT

Verse 18 continues, "By means of all prayer and petition, praying at every time in spirit and watching unto this in all perseverance and petition concerning all the saints." In order to slay the enemy, we must pray. If we do not pray in the spirit, we cannot fight the battle for God. Therefore, the slaying Spirit is the praying Spirit.

As an introduction to the book of Ephesians, Paul tells us that all the blessings to the church are spiritual. Then he goes on to say that the Spirit of the Body is the sealing Spirit and the pledge within us. The indwelling Spirit within us is the seal to testify that we are God's inheritance, and He is also the earnest, the pledge, to guarantee that God is our portion. After this, Ephesians goes on to show us the different aspects of the work of the indwelling Spirit in us. First, He reveals the divine things to us, joins us together as one, and builds us up together as the Body. Then He does the finer, deeper work of strengthening our spirit to renew our soul and fill our whole being. He also equips and qualifies us for the battle. He becomes the slaying Spirit within us so that we pray in Him, and He is the praying Spirit to fight the battle for God in order to fulfill God's purpose. We need to pray concerning all these points in the presence of the Lord. He is the revealing Spirit, the uniting Spirit, the building Spirit, the strengthening Spirit, the renewing Spirit, the filling Spirit, the slaying Spirit, and the praying Spirit. This is the revelation of the Spirit of the Body and for the Body.

CHAPTER EIGHT

THE ALL-INCLUSIVE SPIRIT IN PHILIPPIANS AND THE LOVE IN THE SPIRIT AND SPIRITUAL WISDOM IN COLOSSIANS

Scripture Reading: Phil. 1:19-21, 5-7, 27; 2:5-8, 1; 3:3, 7-11; 4:11-13; Col. 1:8-9; 3:16; 2:5

In the book of Galatians the Spirit is for us to take Christ as our life and live Him, and in Ephesians the Spirit is for the Body life. Between these two books, the revelation of Christ as the Spirit may seem complete. However, these books do not give us the secret of how to apply Christ as our life. Therefore, after these books we have Philippians, which reveals the secret of experiencing Christ as our life and everything. Philippians contains not merely doctrinal teachings but the different aspects of the experience of Christ. In Philippians, Christ is the all-inclusive Spirit for our experience. In chapter 1, Christ is our expression, and we magnify Him in any kind of circumstance (vv. 20-21). In chapter 2, Christ is our pattern and example (vv. 5-8). In chapter 3, Christ is our aim and goal, the One whom we pursue and toward whom we press (vv. 7-11). Then in chapter 4, Christ is not only our outward pattern for us to follow but our inward power, empowering us all the time in every circumstance (v. 13). We need to read Philippians with the point of view that Christ is our expression, pattern, aim, and power. In all these matters, the way, the secret, of experiencing Christ is the all-inclusive Spirit.

The experience of Christ in Philippians is mostly in four aspects, related to our circumstances, the unbelievers, the believers, and God. First, we magnify Christ in any kind of circumstance, condition, state, or situation, whether through

life or through death. We overcome all the troubles and hardships, and nothing can oppress, depress, suppress, or overcome
us. Second, in order to magnify Christ, we need to preach and
impart Him to the unbelievers, presenting Him as the good
tidings. This is the reason that this book mentions the preaching of the gospel, the good work begun by the Lord in us
(1:5-7, 12-14, 18, 27). Third, in order to magnify Christ, we
must fellowship with the believers. This is more glorious. We
present Christ and impart Him to the unbelievers, and we
also serve Him to the believers, fellowshipping the glorious
Christ with one another. In this way the experience of Christ
is related both to the unbelievers and the believers. Fourth,
we magnify Christ by serving and worshipping by the Spirit
of God (3:3).

At the time he wrote this Epistle, the apostle Paul was
in prison where he suffered much. Because the Philippian
believers were concerned for the apostle and because the
church in Philippi had been raised up by Paul, they had fellowship with him in his affliction (4:14). The Philippians also
had fellowship and cooperation in the spreading, the advance,
of the gospel. In addition, Paul spoke of "fellowship of spirit"
(2:1). Paul needed fellowship in prison, and the Philippians
also needed fellowship in spirit. As the children of God, all the
believers need fellowship with one another. Moreover, we also
need to worship God in a proper way. Therefore, in order to
experience Christ, we must magnify Christ in every kind of
circumstance, present Christ to the unbelievers, fellowship
Christ with the believers, and worship God in Christ and with
Christ.

LIVING CHRIST BY THE BOUNTIFUL SUPPLY
OF THE SPIRIT OF JESUS CHRIST

Verse 19 of chapter 1 says, "For I know that for me this
will turn out to salvation through your petition and the bountiful supply of the Spirit of Jesus Christ." In the whole Bible
only this verse speaks of the bountiful supply of the Spirit of
Jesus Christ. Whatever happened to Paul turned out to his
salvation. It was not a damage or a loss to him but a salvation because of the bountiful supply of the Spirit of Jesus

Christ. By this supply Paul could magnify Christ in any kind of situation and under any kind of circumstance. Verses 20 and 21 continue, "According to my earnest expectation and hope that in nothing I will be put to shame, but with all boldness, as always, even now Christ will be magnified in my body, whether through life or through death. For to me, to live is Christ and to die is gain." Paul was put to shame in nothing because whether through life or through death Christ was magnified in his body through the bountiful supply of the Spirit of Jesus Christ. To him, everything was glorious, whether to live or to die. It is only by the bountiful supply of the Spirit of Jesus Christ that to live is Christ and to die is gain.

THE SPIRIT OF GOD, THE SPIRIT OF JESUS, THE SPIRIT OF CHRIST, AND THE SPIRIT OF JESUS CHRIST

Romans 8:9 says, "You are not in the flesh, but in the spirit, if indeed the Spirit of God dwells in you. Yet if anyone does not have the Spirit of Christ, he is not of Him." This verse speaks of the Spirit of God and the Spirit of Christ. Acts 16:7 says, "When they had come to Mysia, they tried to go into Bithynia, yet the Spirit of Jesus did not allow them." Then as we have seen, Philippians 1:19 says, "The Spirit of Jesus Christ." The Spirit of God, the Spirit of Jesus, the Spirit of Christ, and the Spirit of Jesus Christ are not four different Spirits. All these are one Spirit, who is called by four different titles.

Please refer to the diagram on page 80. God was in eternity past, and in time He was incarnated to be a man by the name of Jesus. One day this Jesus went to the cross, and as a man He died and was buried. Following this, He was resurrected, which means that He was glorified and shown to be the very Christ of God (Luke 24:26, 46; Acts 3:13a, 15). In incarnation He became Jesus, and in resurrection He was declared to be the Christ of God. Moreover, this Christ in resurrection became the Spirit (1 Cor. 15:45b; 2 Cor. 3:17). Therefore, we have God, Jesus, Christ, and the Spirit.

The Spirit before the incarnation was simply the Spirit of God. When Jesus was on the earth, He was a man, but within

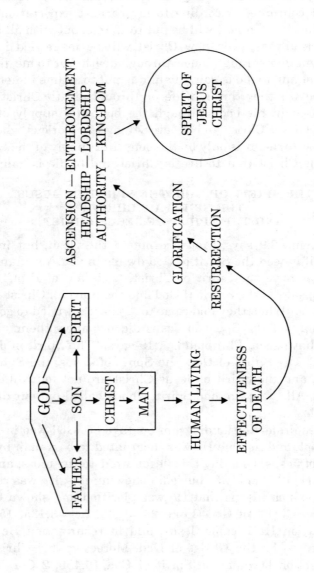

GOD — SON — SPIRIT

FATHER

CHRIST — MAN

HUMAN LIVING

EFFECTIVENESS OF DEATH

RESURRECTION

GLORIFICATION

ASCENSION — ENTHRONEMENT
HEADSHIP — LORDSHIP
AUTHORITY — KINGDOM

SPIRIT OF JESUS CHRIST

THE SPIRIT IN PHILIPPIANS AND COLOSSIANS   81

Him was the reality of God. Thus, the Spirit of Jesus refers to
the Spirit of the incarnated Savior who, as Jesus in His humanity, passed through human living and death on the cross. The
Spirit of Jesus is the suffering, enduring, and forbearing
Spirit, the Spirit of a proper human living. It is by the Spirit
that Jesus was able to live a proper human life, suffering
much, enduring hardships, and bearing all the persecutions.
Then after His resurrection and ascension, this Jesus was
designated as the Christ (Acts 2:36). Today this Christ is the
Spirit, who is called the Spirit of Christ. All the foregoing
terms speak of the history of the Spirit of God, who today is
the Spirit of Jesus Christ.

The Spirit of God, the Spirit of Jesus, the Spirit of Christ,
and the Spirit of Jesus Christ are not four Spirits but one
Spirit in several stages. In the first stage, the Spirit of God
was God alone. In the second stage, God became the man Jesus
so that the Spirit of Jesus could be the Spirit of the incarnated Savior. In the third stage, He was designated the Christ
in resurrection and ascension so that He may be the Spirit
of Christ. Taken all together, He is now the Spirit of Jesus
Christ. Within Him is everything, including God, man, and
the power to suffer, endure, and forbear. Within Him also there
is resurrection power, transcending power, surpassing power,
and overcoming power (Eph. 1:19-22). Also, within Him there
is even the reality of glorification.

Acts 16 speaks of the Spirit of Jesus, not the Spirit of
Christ as in Romans 8. This is because the events in Acts
were a matter of suffering. The apostle Paul went out to preach
the gospel, which involves suffering, hardships, and persecutions. This requires the Spirit of Jesus, who is the enduring,
forbearing, suffering, and longsuffering Spirit. In order to
preach the gospel, we need the Spirit of the man Jesus as the
suffering power. Romans 8, however, deals with the resurrection life. In order to live out the resurrection life, we need the
Spirit of Christ, who is the resurrecting, transcending, surpassing, and overcoming Spirit. We cannot interchange Acts 16
and Romans 8. It would not be right to say that the Spirit of
Christ directed Paul in preaching the gospel, nor is it accu-
rate to speak of the Spirit of Jesus in the context of Romans 8.

In hardship and persecution we need the Spirit of Jesus, and to live out the resurrection life we need the Spirit of Christ.

Philippians 1:19 goes on to speak of the Spirit of Jesus Christ. At that time the writer, the apostle Paul, was in a prison, suffering yet having the expectation that he would magnify Christ. In order to suffer, he needed the Spirit of Jesus, but in order to magnify Christ, he needed the Spirit of Christ. Paul seemed to be saying, "I am now in prison. You Philippians should not be disappointed by this. I have the Spirit of Jesus in order to suffer, endure, and forbear every kind of hardship. I also have the Spirit of Christ to release me, resurrect me, and cause me to transcend to the heavenly places so that I may magnify Christ. I do not care whether I am in life or in death, because I have the transcending, surpassing, overcoming Spirit within me. I have the all-inclusive, bountiful supply of the Spirit of Jesus Christ."

In his translation of the Epistles of Paul, Conybeare tells us that the phrase *bountiful supply* in Greek has a specific meaning, referring to the supplying of all the needs of the chorus by the choragus, the leader of the chorus. The choragus would supply everything the chorus needed, including clothing, food, drink, and instruments. This was the all-inclusive supply of the choragus for the chorus. Today the Spirit of Jesus Christ supplies us with everything we need. We should not consider the apostle as a mere prisoner at that time. Rather, he was part of a heavenly, spiritual "chorus" with the Spirit as his Choragus to afford him a bountiful supply. The Spirit today is not only the Spirit of God, the Spirit of Jesus, or the Spirit of Christ. He is the Spirit of Jesus Christ, the all-inclusive Spirit. Therefore, He affords us the all-inclusive bountiful supply. He is the secret for us to experience Christ.

MAGNIFYING CHRIST
IN EVERY KIND OF CIRCUMSTANCE
BY THE ONE WHO EMPOWERS US

Philippians 4:11-13 says, "Not that I speak according to lack, for I have learned, in whatever circumstances I am, to be content. I know also how to be abased, and I know how to abound; in everything and in all things I have learned the secret both to be filled and to hunger, both to abound and to lack. I am able to do all things in Him who empowers me." We must learn the secret of how to endure any kind of suffering or circumstance. To be poor or to be rich, to be persecuted or to be honored, are all the same to us if we have learned the secret of remaining in any state in order to magnify Christ by the bountiful supply of the Spirit of Jesus Christ. To be abased and to abound include being poor and being rich. Some people do not know how to be poor. When they are poor, they do not know what to do. Others, however, know how to be poor, but they do not know how to be rich. When they become rich, they become foolish. The apostle Paul knew both how to be poor and how to be rich, how to be abased and how to abound, not only in one thing but in everything and in all things.

In verse 12 Paul says, "In everything and in all things I have learned the secret," and in 1:20 he says, "Christ will be magnified in my body, whether through life or through death." As persons existing on this earth and living among humanity, we cannot escape our circumstances. Every day we encounter certain situations. If we prefer not to live in one place, we may have more difficult circumstances when we move to another place. In order to be a normal believer living in the spirit, we must first deal with our circumstances. We should praise the Lord and thank Him for His sovereignty and wisdom. The sovereign, wise hand of the Lord always arranges our circumstances for us and assigns them to us. If we need a wife, He will assign a proper, suitable wife, and if we need a certain kind of child, He will give us one. He also knows what kind of health we need, and He assigns it to us. We should not complain, because all things are under His sovereign and wise hand. The Lord knows what we need, He is never wrong, and He assigns to us our circumstances. Therefore, in order to live in the spirit by Christ as our life, we must learn the secret of how to deal with our circumstances, how to be abased and how to abound, and how to be poor and how to be rich. Then we will be able to magnify Christ.

Paul had learned the secret, and he could do all things, not in himself but in Him who empowered him. We may illustrate this with electrical appliances, which are able to operate because of the empowering of electricity. The One who empowers us in this way is the empowering Spirit. Regardless of the circumstance or state we are in, we can do all things in Him who empowers us so that He may be magnified in our body. This is the experience of Christ as the all-inclusive Spirit so that He may be magnified in any kind of circumstance.

ENJOYING CHRIST THROUGH THE FELLOWSHIP UNTO THE FURTHERANCE OF THE GOSPEL

Verses 5 and 6 of chapter 1 say, "For your fellowship unto the furtherance of the gospel from the first day until now, being confident of this very thing, that He who has begun in you a good work will complete it until the day of Christ Jesus." The fellowship of the gospel is the cooperation in the preaching of the gospel, and the good work in us is the spreading, the furtherance, of the gospel. Verse 27 says, "Only, conduct yourselves in a manner worthy of the gospel of Christ, that whether coming and seeing you or being absent, I may hear of the things concerning you, that you stand firm in one spirit, with one soul striving together along with the faith of the gospel." If we intend to magnify Christ, we must not only overcome every kind of circumstance, but we must also preach the gospel to present Christ to the unbelievers. The all-inclusive Spirit within us constantly supplies us for preaching the gospel. In order to experience Christ and enjoy the bountiful supply of the Spirit, we need to do the work of preaching the gospel. The more we preach the gospel to present Christ to people, the more we will enjoy the bountiful supply of the all-inclusive Spirit within us. On the other hand, if we do not preach the gospel, we will suffer the loss of the supply of the all-inclusive Spirit. In order to enjoy the all-inclusive supply of the Spirit, we need to "spend" the supply. If we do not spend the supply we have received, a further supply will not come.

If we open ourselves to present Christ to the unbelievers, we will realize that within us is a bountiful supply constantly affording us an enjoyment. To preach the gospel is an enjoyment. If we do not preach the gospel, we will not be able to enjoy the all-inclusive Spirit to a greater extent. The more we present Christ to others, the more we will gain Him. The more we "spend" Christ on others, the more Christ we will enjoy. This is the good work begun within us, and this is the fellowship, the cooperation, in the gospel.

OPENING OURSELVES TO HAVE FELLOWSHIP OF SPIRIT

Verse 1 of chapter 2 says, "If there is therefore any encouragement in Christ, if any consolation of love, if any fellowship of spirit, if any tenderheartedness and compassions." As for the unbelievers, we present Christ to them as the gospel. Concerning the believers, though, we need to fellowship. In order to fellowship with the brothers and sisters, we need to open to them to let the Spirit flow out of us, and we should help them to open to us so that the Spirit will flow out of them into us. This is a two-way traffic, a flowing out and a flowing in.

Many Christians find it difficult to open, even in the meetings. In our prayer meetings, for example, it is mostly the same persons who pray every time, and certain others are accustomed to being silent. During the prayer, I may inwardly say to the Lord, "O Lord, open the mouths and release the spirits of more of the brothers and sisters." We should not be afraid of fellowshipping by speaking in the meetings. In a family it is not always the older members who should speak. The family also enjoys hearing the children speak. The older brothers and sisters should give the opportunity to the younger ones to open their mouths to fellowship in the meetings.

Verse 1 speaks of "fellowship of spirit." This spirit is the mingled spirit, the divine Spirit mingled with our human spirit. The secret to opening up in fellowship and helping others to open is the mingled spirit. The more we are in our mind and our feelings, the more we will be silent. We may even consider that the wise way is to remain silent. However, the more we reject our natural mind, consideration, and feelings and turn to the mingled spirit, the more we will open our mouths to fellowship. Even if we do not know what to say, at least we can say, "Praise the Lord. Hallelujah! Christ is Victor." It is even sweeter and more refreshing if the younger ones among us praise the Lord in this way. Because I frequently speak in the meetings, I prefer to remain silent at times so that we may hear something from the other brothers and sisters. We need more fellowship of spirit.

To fellowship is to open ourselves. Fellowship is a current or flow, like that of a stream. Again, we may illustrate this with electricity. There is a kind of fellowship among the electrical lamps in a building, which is the current of electricity that flows within them. In the same way, the Spirit flows out of us, into others, and back to us. Therefore, when we come to the meetings, we need to learn to open to everyone and to help them to open to us. Then we will have a flowing stream among us. This flowing stream in the spirit is fellowship. We need this kind of "fellowship of spirit." If we remain in our soul, the fellowship stops, but if we turn to the spirit, we immediately sense the flowing in the spirit. Then when we follow that flow in the spirit to speak something to one another, we are in the fellowship.

SERVING BY THE SPIRIT OF GOD

Verse 3 of chapter 3 says, "We are the circumcision, the ones who serve by the Spirit of God and boast in Christ Jesus and have no confidence in the flesh." As we have seen, we need to experience Christ in four aspects. As to our circumstances, we magnify Christ in any situation. In whatever happens to us, we must remember that within us there is the all-inclusive Spirit supplying us all the time. It is by Him that we are able to magnify Christ. Second, as to the unbelievers, we preach the gospel by presenting Christ to them. Third, concerning the believers, we have fellowship of spirit. Now as to God, we serve by the Spirit. This is the way to experience Christ.

In verse 3 Paul gives us a contrast between serving God by the Spirit and by the flesh. According to chapter 3, Paul had many virtues to boast of according to the flesh (vv. 4-6). However, he learned the lesson not to serve God by the virtues of the flesh. He gave up all these things and left no ground for them in his service to God. Instead, he learned to serve God by the Spirit. According to the context of this chapter, to serve God by the Spirit is a matter of the resurrection life (v. 10). The Spirit is the reality of the power of resurrection. As we have seen, the Spirit today is no longer only the Spirit of God;

He is the Spirit of Jesus Christ, which includes both human suffering and resurrection. Resurrection power is nothing less than the Spirit Himself. To worship and serve God by the Spirit is to worship and serve in the resurrection power, not in anything natural, in the flesh, or by our self. Paul had virtues in the flesh of which he could boast, but he had seen the vision and learned the secret to give up the good flesh and worship God simply and absolutely in the power of Christ's resurrection. This is the meaning of serving God by the Spirit.

THE GRACE OF THE LORD JESUS CHRIST BEING WITH OUR SPIRIT

The last verse of Philippians says, "The grace of the Lord Jesus Christ be with your spirit" (4:23). The grace of the Lord Jesus Christ is God in Christ as our supply and enjoyment, conveyed to us and realized through the bountiful supply of the Spirit of Jesus Christ. This grace which is the supply of the Spirit is the riches of Christ. The all-inclusive Spirit constantly supplies us with the riches of Christ as grace for our enjoyment. It is by this grace, this supply, that we magnify Christ in every kind of circumstance, present Christ to the unbelievers, fellowship with the believers, and worship God. We must do everything in this grace, which is the bountiful supply of the Spirit of Jesus Christ. Moreover, this grace is with our spirit. In order to enjoy and participate in this grace by magnifying Christ, preaching the gospel, fellowshipping with the believers, and serving God by the Spirit, we need to turn to our spirit and exercise our spirit. Then grace will flow in our spirit as living water. This is to come forward to the throne of grace that we may receive mercy and find grace for timely help (Heb. 4:16).

When we remain in the soul, we are not able to fellowship with the believers, nor can we preach the gospel in a prevailing way. We need to preach the gospel in the spirit. We should not give people merely good doctrinal teaching. We need to give them the living Spirit. When we get into the spirit, people will be saved. To serve God is in the same principle. When we remain in the soul, it is difficult to serve God properly. We need to reject our natural self and soul and turn to the spirit. Right away in the spirit there will be a tendency to serve God. The grace of the Lord Jesus Christ is the flow, the all-inclusive supply, of the Spirit, and this grace, flow, and supply is with our spirit. Therefore, we must turn to our spirit all the time.

In the book of Philippians, the Spirit is the Spirit of the bountiful supply. He is the supplying Spirit who renders and affords us the all-inclusive supply that suffices for us to magnify Christ under any kind of circumstance, present Christ to the unbelievers, fellowship with the saints, and serve God. The Spirit of the bountiful supply constantly supplies us with whatever we need.

LOVE IN THE SPIRIT AND SPIRITUAL WISDOM AND UNDERSTANDING IN COLOSSIANS

Because the book of Colossians emphasizes the Christ who is all and in all, there is little mention of the Spirit in this book. Verses 8 and 9 of chapter 1 say, "Who also has made known to us your love in the Spirit. Therefore we also, since the day we heard of it, do not cease praying and asking on your behalf that you may be filled with the full knowledge of His will in all spiritual wisdom and understanding." Verse 8 speaks of love in the Spirit, verse 9 speaks of spiritual wisdom, and 3:16 mentions spiritual songs. Christ is all and in all to us, but we need spiritual wisdom, the wisdom of the Spirit in our spirit, in order to know all the things of Christ. Moreover, we need love in the Spirit to live out what we know. Therefore, in order to know Christ we need to be in the spirit, and in order to live out Christ, we need the love of the Spirit. It is in the spirit that we have the wisdom to know Christ, and it is by the Spirit that we have the love to live out Christ. Then 2:5 says, "Even though I am absent in the flesh, yet in the spirit I am with you, rejoicing and seeing your order and the solid basis of your faith in Christ." This refers to the human spirit indwelt by the Holy Spirit. May we all be brought into a full realization of the Spirit of Jesus Christ with the bountiful, all-inclusive supply to meet all our needs, and may we experience the Spirit to know Christ and live out Christ.

CHAPTER NINE

THE SANCTIFYING SPIRIT
IN 1 AND 2 THESSALONIANS

Scripture Reading: 1 Thes. 1:5-6, 8; 4:8; 5:19; 2 Thes. 2:13;
1 Thes. 3:13; 4:3-4, 7; 5:21-23, 26; 2 Thes. 1:10a

The first group of the Epistles is Romans through 2 Thessalonians, and the second group is 1 Timothy through Jude. All these Epistles reveal various aspects of the indwelling and life-imparting Spirit. First Thessalonians 1:5 and 6 say, "Our gospel did not come to you in word only, but also in power and in the Holy Spirit and in much assurance, even as you know what kind of men we were among you for your sake. And you became imitators of us and of the Lord, having received the word in much affliction with joy of the Holy Spirit." These verses indicate that the preaching of the gospel must be in the Holy Spirit, and the receiving of the gospel must be also in the Holy Spirit.

Verse 8 of chapter 4 says, "Consequently, he who rejects, rejects not man but God, who also gives His Holy Spirit to you." First, the gospel was preached to the Thessalonians in the Holy Spirit, and they received it by the Holy Spirit. Then God gave them the Holy Spirit. In 5:19 Paul says, "Do not quench the Spirit." The Spirit causes our spirit to be burning (Rom. 12:11), and fanning into flame the gift of God is related to our spirit (2 Tim. 1:6-7). Hence, to quench the Spirit is related to the mingled spirit, the Holy Spirit mingled with our human spirit. Then in 2 Thessalonians 2:13 Paul says, "We ought to thank God always concerning you, brothers beloved of the Lord, because God chose you from the beginning unto salvation in sanctification of the Spirit and belief of the truth." The foregoing are the verses in these two books that are related to the Spirit.

THE HOLY SPIRIT BEING FOR OUR SANCTIFICATION

Sanctification Being the Subject of the Epistles to the Thessalonians

First Thessalonians 3:13 helps us to see the subject of these two Epistles. This verse says, "So that He may establish your hearts blameless in holiness before our God and Father at the coming of our Lord Jesus with all His saints." Here Paul says "saints," not merely "believers." The words *holy, holiness, sanctification,* and *saints* all come from the same root in Greek. The saints are those people who are holy. Then 4:3 and 4 say, "This is the will of God, your sanctification: that you abstain from fornication; that each one of you know how to possess his own vessel in sanctification and honor." Verse 7 continues, "For God has not called us for uncleanness but in sanctification." In chapter 5, verses 21 through 23 say, "Prove all things. Hold fast to what is good; abstain from every kind of evil. And the God of peace Himself sanctify you wholly, and may your spirit and soul and body be preserved complete, without blame, at the coming of our Lord Jesus Christ." Verse 26 continues, "Greet all the brothers with a holy kiss." Finally, 2 Thessalonians 1:10a says, "He comes to be glorified in His saints." All of these verses show us that the Spirit in 1 and 2 Thessalonians is the sanctifying Spirit.

The Holy Spirit Being for the Incarnation of Christ

The Bible uses the different titles of the Holy Spirit in a very meaningful way. As we have seen, 1 Thessalonians 1 says that the gospel came to the Thessalonians not in word only but in the Holy Spirit, they received it in the Holy Spirit, and God gave them the Holy Spirit. The title *Holy Spirit* is not found in the Old Testament. In Psalm 51:11 David says, "Do not cast me from Your presence, / And do not take the Spirit of Your holiness away from me." Similarly, Isaiah 63:10 and 11 say, "They rebelled and grieved / His Spirit of holiness; /

Therefore He turned to become their enemy; / He fought against them. / Then He remembered the days of old, Moses and His people: / Where is He who brought them up out of the sea / With the shepherds of His flock? / Where is He who put in their midst / His Spirit of holiness." In each of these verses, the Hebrew text uses the title *Spirit of Your holiness,* or *His Spirit of holiness,* not *Holy Spirit* as is translated in the King James Version.

The title *Holy Spirit* is first used in relation to the incarnation of the Lord Jesus. Luke 1:35 says, "The angel answered and said to her, The Holy Spirit will come upon you, and the power of the Most High will overshadow you; therefore also the holy thing which is born will be called the Son of God." This transpired at the time of the conception of the Lord Jesus in the womb of a human virgin. Similarly, Matthew 1:20 says, "While he pondered these things, behold, an angel of the Lord appeared to him in a dream, saying, Joseph, son of David, do not be afraid to take Mary your wife, for that which has been begotten in her is of the Holy Spirit." According to a principle in the Bible, the first mention of a name or item gives us the definition, meaning, and governing principle of that item. Accordingly, the title *Holy Spirit* is related to the incarnation.

The incarnation was greater than God's work of creation. In creation God brought millions of items into existence, but in incarnation the Creator brought Himself, the holy One, into His creation. This was accomplished by the Holy Spirit. The last phrase of Luke 1:35 says, "The holy thing which is born will be called the Son of God." This may be translated literally from the Greek as, "The thing which is born will be called Holy, the Son of God." The One brought forth from Mary's womb was called Holy, because He was conceived by the Holy Spirit.

In 1 Thessalonians 1:5-6 and 4:8, the title *Holy Spirit* is used in a strong way. It can also be translated literally from the Greek as "the Spirit, the Holy." Just as we may say "the Eternal" or "the Divine," referring to the eternal One or the divine One, "the Holy" refers to the holy One. This construction is similar to that in 1 John 1:2, in which *the eternal life* may be translated as "the life, the eternal," indicating that the essence of eternity is the divine life. Just as without the divine life we can have nothing eternal, without the Spirit we cannot have holiness. This is the principle of the title *Holy Spirit*. The Spirit in whom the apostles brought the gospel and whom the Thessalonians received is the holy One, the Holy Spirit.

The Principle of Incarnation Being to Make Man Holy by God Coming into Him

The principle of incarnation is that God comes into man to mingle Himself with man. By incarnation the Holy Spirit, the holy One, comes into man, the common one, to make man holy. In the whole universe only God Himself is holy (Rev. 15:4). Thus, before the incarnation none among the human race was holy. All the descendants of the race of Adam are not only sinful but also common. By coming into man to mingle Himself with man and be one with man, God makes man holy. Because of this, the Spirit of God became the Holy Spirit, the One who sanctifies man and makes him holy. In former centuries, Christians considered holiness mainly to be sinlessness. However, in the last thirty years the Lord has shown us that holiness is God Himself, the holy One, coming into common man to make man holy. This is the work of the Holy Spirit.

When the divine Spirit inspired the writers of the Bible, He was very careful and meaningful in the use of words, including the divine titles. Acts 16:6 and 7 say, "They passed through the region of Phrygia and Galatia, having been forbidden by the Holy Spirit to speak the word in Asia. And when they had come to Mysia, they tried to go into Bithynia, yet the Spirit of Jesus did not allow them." On the one hand, verse 6 speaks of the Holy Spirit for the preaching of the word. On the other hand, verse 7 speaks of the Spirit of Jesus, in whom is not only the divine element of God but the human element of Jesus for the apostle's preaching ministry, a ministry accompanied by suffering, hardships, poverty, and persecution. To those who preach, the Spirit is the Spirit of Jesus for suffering in the work, but to those who receive our preaching, He is the Holy Spirit bringing the gospel to them and bringing God into them. Our preaching of the gospel is the work of the

Holy Spirit to bring God into man. The gospel came to the Thessalonians in the Holy Spirit, they received it in the Holy Spirit, God gave them the Holy Spirit, and this Spirit, the holy One, carried out the work of sanctification within them to make them holy. All this gives us the proper understanding of the title *Holy Spirit*. This very meaningful title indicates that He is the sanctifying Spirit, the One who brings God into us and works God into us to make us holy.

God was in eternity, and one day He was incarnated to be a man. In this incarnation the Spirit of God was the Holy Spirit to bring God into man to make man holy, that is, to sanctify man. Then He went to the cross, died, was buried, and resurrected. Now He is the life-giving Spirit to impart life into man in resurrection. In our experience, being made holy by incarnation and by life-imparting are two aspects of one thing. When a sinner receives the gospel, he receives Christ into him. This is a kind of incarnation. Originally he did not have God; thus, he was common and had nothing holy within him. By receiving Christ, God was "incarnated" in him. To receive the gospel is to receive not only the life of God but God Himself. Through the redemption of Christ, God Himself comes into us to make us holy, that is, to sanctify us. Moreover, it is by the Holy Spirit that this gospel is brought to us, and it is by this Holy Spirit that we receive the gospel. Then when we receive the gospel, God gives us the Holy Spirit that He may do the work of sanctification in us to make us holy.

THE SCRIPTURAL MEANING OF SANCTIFICATION

To Be Freed from Sin

As we have seen, the Scriptures convey differing meanings by the different titles of the Spirit. In the two books of Thessalonians, the Spirit is mentioned mainly as the Holy Spirit, and His work within us is related mainly to sanctification, the work of making us holy as God is holy. To be holy should not be considered merely as being sinless. In the Bible, to be holy, to be sanctified, is much more than this. According to a careful reading of the New Testament, to be sanctified includes at least five items. First, it is to be set free from sin.

Romans 6:19 says, "Just as you presented your members as slaves to uncleanness and lawlessness unto lawlessness, so now present your members as slaves to righteousness unto sanctification." In this verse sanctification is in contrast to lawlessness. Then verse 22 says, "But now, having been freed from sin and enslaved to God, you have your fruit unto sanctification, and the end, eternal life." These two verses make it clear that the first aspect of sanctification is to be freed from sin.

To Be Separated from the World unto God

Second, to be sanctified is to be separated from the world, that is, from all things other than God. Anything other than God is the world, the cosmos, the satanic system. John 17:15 through 17 say, "I do not ask that You would take them out of the world, but that You would keep them out of the hands of the evil one. They are not of the world, even as I am not of the world. Sanctify them in the truth; Your word is truth." According to these verses, to be sanctified is to be separated from the world. This does not mean that we are kept away from the world. We are still in the world, but we are not of the world, because we are separated, sanctified, from the world.

According to the history of the Lord's work of recovery, the truth of sanctification was not yet recovered at the time of Martin Luther. At that time it was mainly justification that was recovered. The truth of sanctification began to be recovered at the time of John Wesley, in the eighteenth century. However, only the aspect of being freed from sin was recovered. About one century later, the Brethren in England recovered the second aspect of sanctification—separation from the world. The Brethren pointed out that in Matthew 23:17 and 19 the temple sanctifies the gold and the altar sanctifies the gift, and in 1 Timothy 4:5 our prayer sanctifies our food. The Brethren pointed out that because there is no sin in gold, gifts, or food, to be sanctified must mean something more than being set free from sin. Sanctification is also a separation. When gold is in the homes or market, it is common, but when it is placed in the temple, the temple makes it holy. The temple sanctifies the gold by separating it unto God from all the common gold. It is the same with the gift. When the gift is in our hands, it is common, but when it is placed on the altar, the altar sanctifies it. Similarly, food in the market is common, but when we as believers put it on our table and pray over it, our prayer sanctifies it by separating it unto God for His use. Therefore, to be sanctified is to be separated from anything common unto God to fulfill God's purpose.

To Be Saturated with God's Divine Element

The Lord opened our eyes to see that there is a third aspect of sanctification, which is to be saturated with God's divine element and substance. We may illustrate this with a glass of water. First the water is cleansed from all impurities, and then it is set apart for a particular purpose. However, regardless of how clean and separated it is, it is still only plain water with a natural, clear appearance. As such, it is not yet a full picture of sanctification. We may now add a golden-colored juice into the water, signifying the addition of the divine element of God into us. Eventually the water will be not only cleansed and separated but also saturated with the golden juice, signifying all that God is, the divine "ingredients" of God. To be sanctified is not only to be cleansed from sin and separated from common people. These aspects are only on the negative side. To be sanctified is also something positive. It is to be saturated with God's divine element. In this way we are made holy by the One who alone is holy.

To be sanctified is not merely to have a positional change. It is mainly to have a dispositional change. Together these equal our full sanctification. We are made holy, not only outwardly and positionally but inwardly and dispositionally. Gold is sanctified by the temple only because its position has changed. However, the nature of the gold is not changed in this way. Likewise, food is sanctified by the prayer of the saints only because its position, not its nature, has changed. Our full sanctification is not in this principle. The Holy Spirit within us changes not only our position but also our disposition, our nature within.

Stanza 3 of *Hymns*, #509 says, "The river does the Spirit show, / Coming man's spirit to supply, / That with God's riches he be filled, / Holy to be thereby." The enjoyment of God's riches makes us holy. After we eat food, we assimilate it, and whatever we assimilate saturates us and changes us. Likewise, when we take God as food into us, we assimilate Him as our nourishment, and His substance and element become our "ingredients." It is in this way that we are made holy, that is, sanctified by God and with God as holiness. The way to be sanctified is by taking the Lord as our nourishment. When we feed on Him and drink of Him, we assimilate Him and are sanctified.

To Be Transformed into the Image of God

To be sanctified is also to be transformed into the image of God (Rom. 12:2; 2 Cor. 3:18). We may refer again to the illustration of the water and the golden-colored juice. Before the water was saturated with the juice, it had a plain appearance. However, after being saturated, it is transformed into the same likeness and appearance of the juice. Eventually, we cannot distinguish the water from the juice. In the same way, through sanctification we are being transformed into the likeness, the appearance, of God Himself, and we are being conformed to His image (Rom. 8:29). There is no doubt that John 17 speaks of our separation from the world, but Romans 12:2 and 2 Corinthians 3:18 speak further of a change in our disposition, which is accomplished within us through saturation and permeation with the element of God. In this way, our soul will eventually be transformed, and even our body will be changed through glorification. Then we will be wholly sanctified in our spirit, soul, and body (1 Thes. 5:23). This is the full meaning of sanctification.

To Be Glorified with the Divine Glory

To be sanctified is also to be glorified with the divine glory. One day our physical body will be brought into the glory of God (Rom. 8:23, 30; Phil. 3:21). At that time we will be fully, thoroughly, absolutely, and wholly sanctified (1 Thes. 5:23). We are now under the process of sanctification, but at that time our sanctification will be fully accomplished. Second Thessalonians 1:10 says that the Lord Jesus will come to be glorified in His saints. When we as the saints are thoroughly, fully, wholly sanctified, the Lord Jesus will be glorified in us. We will all be brought into the divine glory, and the Lord Jesus will be glorified in us in that glory. This is a great matter. In 1935 we began to see the third aspect of sanctification, and within ten more years we began to see the fourth aspect. However, it is only within the last few years that we have begun to see the last aspect. These five aspects are the full meaning of sanctification.

Romans 1:4 mentions the Spirit of holiness, and 2 Thessalonians 2:13 speaks of sanctification of the Spirit. There is a difference between holiness and sanctification. J. N. Darby helped us to see that holiness is the nature of God, and sanctification is the practical effect produced by holiness in action. On the one hand, we have the Holy Spirit within us, and on the other hand, we have His work of sanctification. The Spirit within us is the Holy Spirit, who is constantly doing the work of sanctification in us to make us holy. God's salvation includes three steps: the regeneration of our spirit, the transformation of our soul, and the transfiguration of our body. It is through the sanctification of the Spirit that we realize God's salvation. At present we are under the process of sanctification; that is, we are being transformed. Eventually we will be glorified, which is to be brought into the glory of God even in our physical body. This will be the completion of God's sanctification. In summary, sanctification includes being set free from sin, being separated from the world, being saturated with the divine element, being transformed into His divine image, and being glorified with the divine glory. This is the work of the sanctifying Spirit in the two books of Thessalonians.

NOT QUENCHING THE SANCTIFYING SPIRIT

First Thessalonians 5:19 says, "Do not quench the Spirit." Because the Spirit mingles with our spirit, and from our spirit He is doing a work of sanctification, to quench the Spirit is to stop His sanctifying work. If we do not quench the Spirit but always go along with Him, we will not need to care about overcoming sins or being separated from the world. There is no need for us to do the work of sanctification ourselves; this is the work of the Holy Spirit. However, we must take care not to hinder His work. We must learn to give the Holy Spirit a free way to do His work with no quenching, hindrance, or restriction. As we cooperate with the sanctifying Spirit and do not quench Him, day by day and hour by hour we will spontaneously be freed from every kind of sin and be separated from the world and all things other than God. Spontaneously we also will be saturated with the divine element and transformed into the divine image. In this way we will be prepared to be glorified at His coming back.

We do not need to try to overcome many things. We must care only for not quenching the Spirit. We should always be reminded not to quench the Spirit. Are you going shopping? Do not quench the Spirit. Are you about to talk to someone? Do not quench the Spirit. Are you about to lose your temper or do something wrong? Do not quench the Spirit. Someone may ask, "Why should I not go to the movies?" We can simply answer, "Do not quench the Spirit." If we simply take care of not quenching the Spirit, the Spirit will care for our sanctification. The Spirit whom we must not quench is the sanctifying Spirit, the Holy Spirit who brought God into Mary's womb to be incarnated there. This is the same Holy Spirit that today is bringing God into us again and again to accomplish His work of sanctification, that is, to saturate us with the divine element, transform us into His divine appearance, and prepare us for His coming back.

At the coming of the Lord, the work of sanctification will be fully and thoroughly completed, causing us to be the saints in whom He is glorified. Today we are the saints, but we are not manifested as saints, because the process of sanctification has not yet been completed in us. We are still under the process of being sanctified. At the coming of the Lord Jesus we will be thoroughly, fully, wholly, and absolutely sanctified. At that time we will be manifested as saints by the Lord Jesus' being glorified in us. Our full sanctification is the work of the Holy Spirit as revealed in the two books of Thessalonians. We not only have holiness within us, but we also have the work of holiness within us, which is sanctification. It is through this sanctification by the Holy Spirit that we are under the process of being fully saved day by day.

BEING SATURATED WITH THE DIVINE ELEMENT FOR OUR FULL SANCTIFICATION

We do not find the word *saturate* in the Bible, related to sanctification. However, we do have the words *transformed, conformed,* and *glorified,* which imply saturation. Without being saturated with the divine element, we cannot be transformed, conformed, and glorified. The work of transformation, conformation, and glorification does not take place objectively, outside of us. Rather, it is very subjective, within us. Therefore, this work requires that we be saturated with the divine element of God. As the Lord saturates us, we are transformed in our soul, conformed to His image, and transfigured in our body, that is, glorified.

First Thessalonians 5:23 says, "The God of peace Himself sanctify you wholly, and may your spirit and soul and body be preserved complete, without blame, at the coming of our Lord Jesus Christ." By the Lord's work of saturation, we will be transformed and glorified; that is, we will be sanctified in our whole spirit, soul, and body. Since the day the Lord came into us, He has been the saturating element within us. We may compare the Lord's saturation to the spreading of ink. If we inject a drop of ink into the center of a ball of cotton, the ink will spread from the center until it saturates and permeates the whole ball. This is a picture of transformation and glorification. The Triune God as glory has been "injected" into us, and He is now waiting for the opportunity to spread, saturate, and permeate our being. First, He came into our spirit; then, He spreads from our spirit into our soul to transform it. Finally, He will spread from our soul even to our body. At the time of our glorification we will experience full redemption, the redemption not only of our spirit and our soul but also of our body (Rom. 8:23).

Ephesians 3:16-17a and 19b say, "That He would grant you, according to the riches of His glory, to be strengthened with power through His Spirit into the inner man, that Christ may make His home in your hearts through faith...that you may be filled unto all the fullness of God." When our inner man, our spirit, is strengthened by the Spirit, we give more room to the Spirit, and Christ takes over and makes His home in all the parts of our heart. As a result, our whole being is filled unto all the fullness of God. This process is our saturation and permeation with God. It is in this way that we are transformed and glorified. The first step of sanctification is that we are kept from sin, and the second is that we are separated from the world. Then we are saturated and permeated within by the Holy Spirit. Gradually we are transformed in our soul, and eventually we will be transfigured in our body, that is, glorified. Glorification is the final, ultimate step of sanctification. At that time we will be wholly and thoroughly sanctified in our spirit, soul, and body. We will be one with the Lord in glory, and we will meet Him in glory at His return. This will be the result of our full sanctification. Today we are under the process of daily sanctification.

BEING WHOLLY SANCTIFIED TO BE IN THE LORD'S PRESENCE AT HIS COMING

The two Epistles to the Thessalonians speak of Christ's second coming (1 Thes. 1:10; 2:19; 3:13; 4:15; 5:23; 2 Thes. 1:10; 2:1). In the foregoing verses, the Greek word for "coming" is *parousia,* which also means "presence." The way to be in the Lord's presence at His coming is by being fully sanctified. We may feel that our condition is acceptable, but if we were to stand in the Lord's presence today, we would lament that too much of our inward being is still not sanctified. Only when we are thoroughly saturated, permeated, and sanctified can we be peaceful in the Lord's presence, because at that time nothing within us will cause us shame. We must be wholly sanctified from within to without, until every inward part is full of Christ and brought into the new creation. Then we will be bold and have the full peace to stand in His parousia, His presence. This is a matter not only of positional sanctification, a change in our position. It is even more a matter of dispositional sanctification, a change in our disposition. We need a change in our nature, our disposition, and our entire being must be transformed.

CHAPTER TEN

THE JUSTIFYING, SPEAKING, AND GUARDING SPIRIT IN 1 AND 2 TIMOTHY, THE RENEWING SPIRIT IN TITUS, AND THE SPIRIT OF GRACE IN PHILEMON

Scripture Reading: 1 Tim. 4:7-8; 3:16; 4:1; 2 Tim. 1:7, 14; 4:22; Titus 3:5-7; Philem. 10, 16, 25

Many people consider the two Epistles to Timothy and the one to Titus to be the "pastoral" Epistles, the books intended to teach certain ones how to "pastor" a church. These books do tell us something about how to take care of a church, but if we spend the time to get into their depths, we will see that this is not their basic thought. The basic thought of these three books is the exercise unto godliness. First Timothy 4:7 and 8 say, "The profane and old-womanish myths refuse, and exercise yourself unto godliness. For bodily exercise is profitable for a little, but godliness is profitable for all things, having promise of the present life and of that which is to come." *Godliness* is a key word in these books (2:2; 3:16; 6:3, 5, 6, 11; 2 Tim. 3:5; Titus 1:1). The word *exercise* in Greek corresponds to the English word *gymnastics*. Just as people exercise in gymnastics for the sake of their body, we need to exercise ourselves unto godliness. Therefore, the Spirit in 1 and 2 Timothy and Titus is the Spirit for the exercise unto godliness.

IN 1 TIMOTHY THE JUSTIFYING OF THE SPIRIT BEING RELATED TO GODLINESS— THE MANIFESTATION OF GOD IN THE FLESH

First Timothy 3:16 says, "Confessedly, great is the mystery of godliness: He who was manifested in the flesh, / Justified in the Spirit, / Seen by angels, / Preached among the nations, /

Believed on in the world, / Taken up in glory." In the Epistles
to Timothy and Titus, the Spirit is mentioned for the first
time in this verse, a verse related to godliness. Godliness is
God manifested in the flesh, that is, God expressed in human
beings. That the man Jesus was God manifested in the flesh
was justified, proved, and vindicated only in the Spirit. The
Spirit constantly vindicated that Jesus was not an ordinary
man but one in whom God was manifested (Matt. 3:16-17;
12:28; Rom. 1:3-4). In the same principle, whenever we are not
doing things in a way that expresses God, the Spirit condemns,
but when we exercise ourselves unto godliness to walk and
live in a way that expresses God, the Spirit justifies, vindicates, that we have godliness. This vindication is not only
within ourselves but in the hearts of those who observe our
saintly walk and life of godliness.

There is no need to proclaim that we manifest God in the
flesh or to try to prove that our life and walk is one of godliness. The Spirit justifies, vindicates, and proves this for us.
We may do things that are very good, but they are not God
Himself. We may love people or show patience, but our love
and patience may not be God; they may only be good. On the
other hand, we may have a love that is not merely good but
is God Himself. Likewise, our patience may give people the
impression not merely that we are good but that we are living
out God. We cannot explain how we know this, but within us
there is something that vindicates, justifies, or proves. The
sense and realization that we have by the vindicating Spirit
within tell us whether someone's love is good or whether it
is God Himself. Sometimes when a brother loves us, we have
the deep sense that this love is not merely something good.
Rather, this brother's love is the expression, the manifestation, of God. The brother is a human being in the flesh, but
his love is the expression of God; it is in godliness, God manifested in the flesh.

It is the same with humility. The submission that a sister
shows to her husband may seem good, but in actuality it may
be with a poor attitude. In such a case, the Spirit indicates
that this submission is of herself and not the expression of
God. We cannot explain with mere words how we sense that

something good is actually poor and out of ourselves. This can be compared to our sense of taste, by which we know what is sweet and what is salty. The Spirit within us is the vindicating Spirit, always vindicating whether or not we live in godliness. By this Spirit we can realize whether or not our love, humility, submission, patience, and goodness are God Himself. This is the meaning of "justified in the Spirit." The Spirit is constantly vindicating what is of God and what is merely out of ourselves.

We may come to a brother to say something good to him, but deep within us we will have the sense that our words are simply from our self; they are not the expression of Christ or the manifestation of God. In this case we do not have godliness but merely a kind of human, sinful morality. The vindicating Spirit proves whether or not we are exercising unto godliness. If we are, the vindicating Spirit will confirm that we are right; otherwise, the Spirit will condemn and protest that we are acting, living, and doing things to express ourselves.

When we love others or submit to them, we may love and submit only for our own glory. No one can tell us this; only the Spirit can vindicate. Brother Watchman Nee once told me, "People can deceive us, but they can never deceive the Spirit." If we are not persons in the Spirit, we can be cheated by others, but if we have the Spirit and are in the Spirit, we cannot be cheated. The more someone loves us, the more we may realize that this love is not godliness, the manifestation and expression of God. Rather, we may sense a wrong motive in this kind of love. The searching Spirit vindicates whether or not we are persons living in the Spirit. In the matter of godliness, He vindicates what is within us, and He vindicates what is in others.

THE SPEAKING AND WARNING SPIRIT

First Timothy 4:1 says, "The Spirit says expressly that in later times some will depart from the faith, giving heed to deceiving spirits and teachings of demons by means of the hypocrisy of men who speak lies, of men who are branded in their own conscience as with a hot iron." Here Paul does not say "the Holy Spirit"; he simply says "the Spirit." Many times in the New Testament this term denotes not only the Spirit Himself but the Spirit mingled with our human spirit. The Spirit in verse 1 is the speaking Spirit, the Spirit who mingles with our spirit and always speaks.

Here the Spirit's speaking is an express, distinct warning concerning those who depart from the faith. For someone's conscience to be branded as with a hot iron means that they have given up the feeling in their conscience; that is, their conscience has lost its function. In this way, the speaking Spirit warns against ungodliness. To depart from the faith, to give heed to deceiving spirits and teachings of demons, and to speak lies in hypocrisy are all ungodliness. The vindicating Spirit speaks to warn us not to pay attention to anything other than godliness. Therefore, the vindicating Spirit in this verse is the speaking and warning Spirit. The Spirit for our exercise unto godliness is not only the vindicating Spirit but also the warning Spirit. Moreover, His speaking is not outside of us; it is an inner speaking, the speaking of the Spirit mingled with our spirit. The Spirit within our spirit warns us to be on the alert, because in the latter days there will be many things contrary to godliness.

THE GUARDING SPIRIT FOR THE GOOD DEPOSIT IN 2 TIMOTHY

Second Timothy 1:14 says, "Guard the good deposit through the Holy Spirit who dwells in us." God has deposited a precious treasure in us, just as we deposit something valuable in a bank. According to the two Epistles to Timothy, this good deposit is the Triune God with all that He has. God has deposited Himself in Christ through the Spirit into us as a treasure. Second Corinthians 4:7 says that this treasure is in earthen vessels. The deposit is a treasure, but the "bank" is worthless and fragile. Therefore, we need to guard the deposit through the Holy Spirit. By ourselves we are not adequate to guard this good deposit, but the Spirit is capable. The Holy Spirit, the holy One who dwells in us, is the guarding Spirit. This guarding is for our exercise unto godliness. The Spirit, the holy One, has brought God into us as the good deposit. Now it is He, not ourselves, through whom we guard this deposit.

According to the Epistles to Timothy, the good deposit is not only the Triune God but also the teaching related to the Triune God. All the proper, healthy teachings are included in this good deposit (1 Tim. 1:10; 2 Tim. 4:3). If we guard the deposit of the Triune God and the healthy teaching, we will know how to minister to others so that they also may realize the Triune God as their good deposit (1 Tim. 4:6).

FULFILLING GOD'S ECONOMY BY THE HOLY SPIRIT WITH OUR HUMAN SPIRIT

Our Human Spirit Being a Spirit of Power and of Love and of Sobermindedness

The above three aspects of the Spirit—justifying, speaking, and guarding—are all for our exercise unto godliness. The Holy Spirit vindicates godliness. He also warns against ungodliness and guards all the things related to godliness. Therefore, it is by Him that we exercise unto godliness. Moreover, for this exercise we need not only the vindicating, speaking, and guarding Holy Spirit but also our regenerated human spirit. Second Timothy 1:7 says, "God has not given us a spirit of cowardice, but of power and of love and of sobermindedness." This is our human spirit with all three parts of the soul under its control. Our spirit, which is at the center of our being, is surrounded by the soul with its three parts—the mind, emotion, and will. In order for the spirit to be released, these three parts must be subdued by the spirit. Then the spirit will become a spirit of power with the will under its control, a spirit of love with the emotion under its control, and a spirit of sobermindedness with the mind under its control. This is a normal and strong spirit. It is not by the Holy Spirit only but also by such a regenerated and renewed human spirit that we exercise ourselves unto godliness to manifest God and express Christ.

The Lord Being with Our Spirit

Verse 22 of chapter 4 says, "The Lord be with your spirit. Grace be with you." We are able and qualified to exercise ourselves unto godliness because God has given us a wonderful, strong, and normal spirit—a spirit of power, love, and sobermindedness with Christ in it. Such a spirit is mingled with the Holy Spirit, who is constantly vindicating, warning, and guarding. Because we have these divine, rich, powerful, and adequate provisions, it is not only possible but even easy for us to exercise unto godliness. There is no excuse for not exercising ourselves unto godliness. By these two spirits—the Holy Spirit with our spirit—we can fulfill God's economy (1 Tim. 1:4).

THE RENEWING SPIRIT FOR
OUR EXERCISE UNTO GODLINESS IN TITUS

Titus 3:5-7 says, "Not out of works in righteousness which we did but according to His mercy He saved us, through the washing of regeneration and the renewing of the Holy Spirit, whom He poured out upon us richly through Jesus Christ our Savior, in order that having been justified by His grace, we might become heirs according to the hope of eternal life." God has given us the Spirit, the holy One, and has poured out this Spirit upon us with the purpose that we may be heirs of the eternal life according to our hope, that is, that we may enjoy the eternal life as our inheritance. Today we are enjoying this life as a foretaste, and in the future we will enjoy this life as the full taste.

The Holy Spirit is continually doing a work to renew us. According to the thought of 1 and 2 Timothy and Titus, this renewing work of the Holy Spirit has much to do with the exercise unto godliness. In order to exercise ourselves unto godliness, we need to realize the renewing work of the indwelling Spirit. The indwelling Spirit is always working to renew us, and under this renewing we are able to exercise ourselves unto godliness.

Titus 3 speaks not only of the renewing of the Holy Spirit but also of the washing of regeneration. The word for *washing* in Greek is the word for *laver*, the vessel in the temple that contained the washing water. *Regeneration* here does not have the same meaning as being born anew in John 3:3. Here the word refers to a change from one state to another. It is a kind of reconditioning, remaking, or remodeling with life. To rebuild a typewriter or remodel a house does not involve life, but the change in condition produced by regeneration requires life. In John 3, life comes into us when we are born again, but in Titus 3 this new life reconditions, remakes, and reconstructs us into a new condition. We all need to be reconditioned, reconstructed, and remade by the new life. This renewing and reconditioning of the Holy Spirit is for our exercise unto godliness. The more we are renewed, reconditioned, and remodeled, the more we express Christ and manifest God, that is, the more we have godliness.

By all that we have said above, we can see that the Epistles to Timothy and Titus are not for us to "pastor" a church. Rather, they are for us to exercise ourselves unto godliness. God's commission and good deposit are not for "pastoring." It is for us to exercise a strong spirit with Christ in it, trusting in the Spirit who justifies, warns, guards, renews, and reconditions. By this Spirit with our regenerated spirit we can exercise unto godliness, imparting and ministering life to others. First Timothy 4:6 says, "If you lay these things before the brothers, you will be a good minister of Christ Jesus, being nourished with the words of the faith and of the good teaching which you have closely followed." *These things* refer to the things related to godliness. A good minister of Jesus Christ is not taught with theology in order to be a pastor of a church. Instead, he is nourished with the words of the faith and of the good teaching. We need to drop the thought of "pastoring" and be filled with the thought of being good ministers of Christ who are nourished in the word. If we are nourished in this way, we will be able to exercise unto godliness.

THE SPIRIT OF GRACE
FOR THE CHURCH LIFE IN PHILEMON

In the book of Philemon, Onesimus was a purchased bondslave who ran away from Philemon, his master. After being captured, he was put into prison with the apostle Paul, and while there, he was saved. This slave became a spiritual child of the apostle Paul and a dear brother in Christ. When Paul realized that he was the slave of Philemon, his fellow worker,

Paul instructed Onesimus to return in peace with this Epistle to his master, with the hope that Philemon would forgive him and also receive him no longer only as a slave but also as a brother (vv. 10, 16).

In the ancient times, a master had the authority to put an escaped slave to death. However, this slave had now become a brother through the apostle who had brought Philemon to the Lord (v. 19) and who was writing to urge Philemon to accept this slave as a dear brother. This required much grace on the part of Philemon. Therefore, the last verse of this Epistle says, "The grace of the Lord Jesus Christ be with your spirit" (v. 25). Paul seemed to be saying, "Philemon, I am asking you not only to forgive him but to receive him back as a dear brother. I know that this is difficult for anyone to do, but I commend you to this good word: the grace of the Lord Jesus Christ be with your spirit. You cannot do this in your flesh or soul, but if you turn to the spirit, grace will be there as the all-inclusive supply of the Spirit of Jesus Christ. By this grace you will be more than able to do what I ask. This grace is infinite, unlimited, and without measure, and it can accomplish anything. I, Paul, have learned the lesson and secret that I can do all things in this grace. Although I have charged you to do something difficult, His grace is sufficient for you."

If a master in the church life can receive his slave as a brother, then he can receive anyone, regardless of their background, situation, condition, or stage of life. This is our need in the church life. In the church there is no Greek and Jew, circumcision and uncircumcision, barbarian, Scythian, slave, or free man, but Christ is all and in all (Col. 3:11). To say this is easy, but to practice it is not. According to a careful study of the Bible and of history, Philemon lived in Colossae, and the church there met in his home (Philem. 2; cf. Col. 4:17; Philem. 10; cf. Col. 1:2; 4:9). This means that in the church meeting Philemon might sit side by side with Onesimus. There was no such custom in the churches that masters sat on one level in the meetings but slaves sat on another. Both the masters and the slaves came together as brothers and sat side by side. This is the proper way of the church life. Therefore, the church life requires an all-sufficient grace. If by grace a master can sit with a slave as a dear brother, then there is nothing he cannot do. We can do all things by the grace in our spirit, which is the all-inclusive Christ for us to have a proper church life. This short Epistle to Philemon is a strong proof of what we can enjoy in the church life by grace.

CHAPTER ELEVEN

THE ETERNAL, TESTIFYING, DISTRIBUTING, AND ANOINTING SPIRIT IN HEBREWS

Scripture Reading: Heb. 9:14, 12, 15; 5:9; 3:7-8; 9:6-8; 10:15; 1:1-2a; 2:4; 10:29; 4:16; 6:4; 1:9; 12:9, 23; 4:12; 10:19

The book of Hebrews tells us that Christ is superior to Judaism and everything related to it. However, if we read this book carefully in the spirit, we will realize that it also deals with the indwelling Spirit. It is not a book of doctrinal teaching; rather, it is a book of experience in our spirit through the Holy Spirit.

THE ETERNAL SPIRIT

Verse 14 of chapter 9 reveals a special title of the Holy Spirit. This verse says, "How much more will the blood of Christ, who through the eternal Spirit offered Himself without blemish to God, purify our conscience from dead works to serve the living God?" This is the only place in the Bible that mentions the eternal Spirit. Verse 12 says that Christ entered into the Holy of Holies, having obtained eternal redemption for us, and verse 15 says that those who have been called might receive the promise of the eternal inheritance. Similarly, 5:9 says, "Having been perfected, He became to all those who obey Him the source of eternal salvation." These eternal items—eternal redemption, the eternal inheritance, and eternal salvation—all take the eternal Spirit as the center.

Judaism is a religion with rituals and regulations in letters, but Christ is a living person with eternal life in the Spirit. The things of Judaism are simply shadows and figures of things to come, but Christ is the reality and the fulfillment of all the shadows and figures in the Old Testament. All these shadows and figures were only temporary and transitory, but Christ as the reality is eternal, perpetual forever. Moreover, the things in Judaism were only in letter, but Christ, the living One, offered Himself to God for eternal redemption by the eternal Spirit so that we may partake of the eternal inheritance. This eternal inheritance is all the riches of the Godhead. By the eternal redemption of Christ, we have the right to the eternal inheritance. By the eternal Spirit, Christ is the Author, the source, and the cause of eternal salvation to us, and we enjoy Him as our eternal salvation. Therefore, in this book the Holy Spirit is the eternal Spirit. In order to experience all that is revealed in this book, we must know how to touch this eternal Spirit.

For something to be eternal does not only mean that it is everlasting. To be eternal spans all time and space and surpasses all time and space. Therefore, eternal redemption is a redemption that is perpetual and eternally effective to meet and surpass all needs throughout all time and space. In the same principle, eternal salvation is not a temporary or transitory salvation. Rather, it meets and surpasses all the needs of all time and space. Likewise, the Spirit is not only the all-inclusive Spirit with all the riches of Christ; He is also the eternal Spirit, who meets all our needs for all time and throughout all space, and His supply surpasses all time and space. This means that there is no need at any time or in any place that He cannot meet.

We have already considered several titles of the Holy Spirit in the New Testament: *the Spirit of God, the Holy Spirit, the Spirit of Jesus, the Spirit of Christ, the Spirit of Jesus Christ,* and *the life-giving Spirit.* Now we see that the Spirit is also the eternal Spirit. These are not seven different Spirits but one Spirit in different stages with different aspects. Please refer once again to the diagram on page 80. In eternity past He was the Spirit of God (Gen. 1:2). Then in order to bring God into man, to bring the holy One into humanity, He was the Holy Spirit (Luke 1:35; Matt. 1:20). Through the human living and death of Jesus, He became the Spirit of Jesus for doing the will of God through suffering and endurance (Acts 16:7). In Christ's designation in resurrection, He became the Spirit of

Christ (Rom. 1:4; 8:9). Through all this inclusively, He is the Spirit of Jesus Christ, the Spirit for suffering in resurrection (Phil. 1:19). For coming into man to impart life to him, He is the life-giving Spirit (1 Cor. 15:45b). Moreover, He is the eternal Spirit, spanning and surpassing all space and time. Through this Spirit, Christ offered Himself to God as an eternal sacrifice to accomplish an eternal redemption that we may enjoy the eternal inheritance. Therefore, He is the source of salvation to us, not a salvation that is temporary, partial, or limited, but one that is eternal to meet all the needs for all time in all space. This is the Spirit unveiled in the book of Hebrews.

THE SPEAKING AND TESTIFYING SPIRIT

The Speaking Spirit for Our Entering into Christ as Our Good Land

Hebrews 3:7-8 says, "Therefore, even as the Holy Spirit says, 'Today if you hear His voice, do not harden your hearts as in the provocation, in the day of trial in the wilderness.'" According to verses 12 to 15, the Holy Spirit says that we need to take heed, be careful, and be on the alert that we do not have an evil heart of unbelief, but rather that we exhort one another. The good land is a type of Christ as our rest, and Joshua as the companion to Caleb is a type of Christ as the One who brings us into the rest. Therefore, we must exhort one another to enter into Christ as our good land and to know Him as our Partner, our Companion (1:9; 3:14). To consider that entering into the rest is too difficult is to have an evil heart of unbelief as the people of Israel had. We must realize that today, as the all-inclusive and eternal Spirit, Christ is available to us. He is our good land, and He is our rest. Moreover, He is also our Joshua. If we would simply be the "Calebs" who have faith, we will enjoy Christ as our Companion to bring us into the rest. Therefore, there is no excuse for us not to enter into the rest.

The Spirit today is speaking in us to assure us that Christ is available as the good land and the rest into which we enter. It is not difficult to enter into the rest because by the eternal

Spirit we are Christ's companions and He is our Companion to bring us into the rest. In this way we partake of Him and enjoy Him to the extent that it is easy to enter in. The Spirit speaks that Christ is so available. To enter into Him is not difficult, because He is not only the land but also the real Joshua. He is not only the rest but also the Companion to bring us into the rest. The Spirit—the holy One and the eternal One—is constantly speaking this within us.

The Testifying Spirit
Making the Things of Christ Clear to Us

Verses 6 and 7 of chapter 9 say, "Now these things having been thus prepared, into the first tabernacle the priests enter continually, accomplishing their worship; but into the second, only the high priest enters, once a year and not without blood, which he offers for himself and for the sins of ignorance of the people." These verses refer to the actions of the priests in the Holy Place and Holy of Holies in the tabernacle. Verse 8 continues, "The Holy Spirit thus making this clear, that the way of the Holy of Holies has not yet been manifested while the first tabernacle still has its standing." If we are in the spirit while we read concerning the things of the tabernacle, the Holy Spirit, the eternal Spirit who is not restricted by time or space, will speak to us and point out to us the real significance of these things.

Verses 11 and 12 say, "Christ, having come as a High Priest of the good things that have come into being, through the greater and more perfect tabernacle not made by hands, that is, not of this creation, and not through the blood of goats and calves but through His own blood, entered once for all into the Holy of Holies, obtaining an eternal redemption." Then verses 14 and 15 say, "How much more will the blood of Christ, who through the eternal Spirit offered Himself without blemish to God, purify our conscience from dead works to serve the living God? And because of this He is the Mediator of a new covenant, so that, death having taken place for redemption of the transgressions under the first covenant, those who have been called might receive the promise of the eternal inheritance." These are not merely words spoken by man. These are the words spoken by the Holy Spirit, showing us how Christ offered Himself to God through the eternal Spirit, opening the way into the Holy of Holies and accomplishing an eternal redemption for us so that we may inherit all the riches of God. When we read these things in the spirit, the Holy Spirit will interpret them to us and point out the various aspects and riches of Christ in them.

Verse 10 of chapter 10 says, "By which will we have been sanctified through the offering of the body of Jesus Christ once for all." Verses 12 through 16 continue, "But this One, having offered one sacrifice for sins, sat down forever on the right hand of God, henceforth waiting until His enemies are made the footstool for His feet. For by one offering He has perfected forever those who are being sanctified. And the Holy Spirit also testifies to us, for after having said, 'This is the covenant which I will covenant with them after those days, says the Lord: I will impart My laws upon their hearts, and upon their mind I will inscribe them.'" While we read and consider the things concerning the work of Christ, the Holy Spirit testifies and witnesses within us that Christ is our High Priest, He has accomplished full redemption, our sins have been taken away, and the way into the Holy of Holies has been opened. His blood is effective, the sacrifice for sin which He offered is perpetual, and we now have boldness through His blood to enter into the Holy of Holies to contact God, obtain mercy, and find grace to meet our timely need. The Spirit who thus testifies is the eternal Spirit through whom Christ offered Himself to God. In this eternal and testifying Spirit we enjoy Christ as the Author of our eternal salvation.

In quoting from the Old Testament, most books of the New Testament tell us which person spoke that word. However, Hebrews never tells us the name of the quoted speaker. Rather, it says that the Holy Spirit testifies. Moreover, the author of Hebrews did not tell us his name, as the writers of the other Epistles do. This is because Hebrews stresses that it is not man but the Holy Spirit who speaks. Verses 1 and 2a of chapter 1 say, "God, having spoken of old in many portions and in many ways to the fathers in the prophets, has at the last of these days spoken to us in the Son." Chapter 1 says that it is God who speaks in the Son, but the following chapters say that it is the Holy Spirit who speaks. This means that God speaks in the Son as the Holy Spirit. When the eternal Spirit speaks in us, that is the speaking of the Son of God. Therefore, whenever we read the Bible—whether Moses, the Psalms, the prophets, or the New Testament apostles—we must receive not only the written word but also the inner speaking of the Holy Spirit. Then we will receive something real from the Word. While we read the black and white letters, there is a living One who speaks in us, pointing out, testifying, and witnessing concerning Christ. This is the work of the eternal Spirit, who spans and surpasses all time and space. Otherwise, whatever we read will be only dead letter to us.

THE DISTRIBUTING SPIRIT AND THE SPIRIT OF GRACE

Verse 4 of chapter 2 says, "God bearing witness with them both by signs and wonders and by various works of power and by distributions of the Holy Spirit according to His will." The distributing Spirit within us dispenses something into us. In principle, the things the Spirit dispenses to us are all the riches of Christ. We should not consider that the gifts of the Spirit include only things such as tongues and healings. According to Romans 12:6-10, even to serve, lead, teach, show mercy, love others, and extend hospitality are gifts, the distributions of the riches of all that Christ is. The eternal Spirit, the holy One, not only speaks to us about Christ and reveals to us the things of Christ, but while He is speaking and revealing, He imparts, distributes, and dispenses the bountiful riches of Christ into us.

Hebrews 10:29 speaks of the "Spirit of grace" (Zech. 12:10), and 4:16 says, "Let us therefore come forward with boldness to the throne of grace that we may receive mercy and find grace for timely help." *The Spirit of grace* is a sweet and precious title. Since grace is nothing less than the riches of Christ Himself, it is only by the Spirit of grace who dispenses the riches of Christ into us that we can find grace. Second Corinthians 13:14 speaks of "the grace of the Lord Jesus Christ and the love of God and the fellowship of the Holy

Spirit." Grace is of Christ, and the fellowship of the Spirit is the transmission of this grace by the Spirit of grace. The eternal Spirit, who is the Spirit of grace, always speaks something of Christ in us and distributes the riches of Christ into us. Hebrews 6:4 says that we have been made "partakers of the Holy Spirit." The Holy Spirit speaks concerning Christ, and He distributes, ministers, the riches of Christ into us as grace. Therefore, we enjoy Him and partake of Him as the Spirit of grace who transmits the grace of Christ to us to meet our timely need.

THE ANOINTING SPIRIT

Verse 9 of chapter 1 says, "You have loved righteousness and hated lawlessness; therefore God, Your God, has anointed You with the oil of exultant joy above Your partners." The Lord Jesus was anointed with the oil of the eternal Spirit. Because God poured out the Spirit of exultant joy upon Him, He could offer Himself to God by this eternal Spirit. The word *Christ* means "the anointed One." By being anointed by the Father with the Spirit of exultant joy, He became the Christ.

THE HUMAN SPIRIT IN THE BOOK OF HEBREWS

The Father of Our Spirits

The book of Hebrews also speaks of our human spirit. Verse 9 of chapter 12 says, "We have had the fathers of our flesh as discipliners and we respected them; shall we not much more be in subjection to the Father of spirits and live?" In regeneration we are born of God in our spirit (John 1:13; 3:6). Hence, God is the Father of our spirits. The context of Hebrews 12 is God's dealing with His sons. God deals with us in our spirit because He is the Father of our spirits.

Being Perfected in the Spirit

Verse 23 says, "To the church of the firstborn, who have been enrolled in the heavens; and to God, the Judge of all; and to the spirits of righteous men who have been made perfect." God perfects righteous men in their spirit. God's dealing with

us is related to our spirit, and His perfecting work is also in
our spirit.

Discerning the Spirit from the Soul

Verse 12 of chapter 4 says, "The word of God is living and
operative and sharper than any two-edged sword, and pierc-
ing even to the dividing of soul and spirit and of joints and
marrow, and able to discern the thoughts and intentions of
the heart." God is the Father of our spirits, the One who deals
with us in our spirit and perfects us in the spirit. Moreover,
Christ Himself as the Spirit is in our spirit (2 Tim. 4:22; Rom.
8:16). Therefore, we need to discern our spirit from our soul.

Entering the Holy of Holies in Our Spirit

Hebrews 10:19 says, "Having therefore, brothers, boldness
for entering the Holy of Holies in the blood of Jesus." This is
not merely the Holy of Holies in the heavens. If the Holy of
Holies were only in heaven, we could not enter into it today
while we are still on this earth. Therefore, this must be the
Holy of Holies in our spirit. The Holy of Holies in our spirit
corresponds with the Holy of Holies in the heavens. In principle, these are two aspects, two ends, of one entity. Subjectively
speaking, the Holy of Holies today is in our spirit. Therefore,
we must discern our spirit from our soul so that we may enter
into the Holy of Holies where Christ, the Ark, the Shekinah
glory of God, and the presence of God are, where we can contact God, obtain mercy, and find grace as the flowing, living
water for us to enjoy. This flowing, living water is simply the
Spirit of grace who transmits the riches of Christ as grace
into our spirit for our enjoyment to meet our timely need.
This is the key to the experience of the things of Christ
revealed in this book. Without the key of our spirit, Christ
would be only objective to us, and we would have no way to
enter into Him.

On the one hand, we need to have an objective vision of
Christ as the One who is superior to Judaism in every aspect.
On the other hand, we must realize that today He is the eter-
nal Spirit, the holy One, who brings Christ into our spirit.
God the Father deals with us in our spirit, so in order to

contact God, experience Christ, and realize the Spirit, we must discern our spirit from our soul. This means that we must always turn to the spirit and divide our spirit from our soul. When we turn to our spirit, we enter into the Holy of Holies. Then we have Christ as the presence of God. We can contact God in all His fullness and enjoy Christ as the tree of life in the flow of the living water (Rev. 22:1-2). The tree of life is Christ as our grace, and the flow of living water is the transmitting Spirit.

Again I say, the key to our experience of Christ in an inner and subjective way is to discern our spirit from our soul and to learn how to turn to the spirit. Whenever we turn to the spirit, we immediately find the flowing of the Spirit of grace who transmits the riches of Christ into us as grace to meet our timely need. This is the key to experiencing all the riches of Christ as revealed in the book of Hebrews.

CHAPTER TWELVE

THE ENVYING SPIRIT, THE SPIRIT OF GLORY, THE PROPHESYING SPIRIT, THE ANOINTING SPIRIT, AND THE SPIRIT OF PRAYER IN JAMES THROUGH JUDE

Scripture Reading: James 4:4-5; 2:26; 1 Pet. 4:14, 17; 1:2, 10-12; 2:5; 3:18-19, 4; 4:6; 2 Pet. 1:21; 1 John 1:3, 7; 2:20, 27; 3:24; 4:13, 1-3, 6; 5:6-8; Jude 19-20

THE ENVYING SPIRIT
AND OUR HUMAN SPIRIT IN JAMES

The Spirit Longing to Envy
That We Would Love God with an Undivided Love

In the book of James, one verse refers to the Holy Spirit and another to our human spirit. Verses 4 and 5 of chapter 4 says, "Adulteresses, do you not know that the friendship of the world is enmity with God? Therefore whoever determines to be a friend of the world is constituted an enemy of God. Or do you think that the Scripture says in vain: 'The Spirit, whom He has caused to dwell in us, longs to envy'?" The indwelling Spirit of God is always longing with envy that we would love God with our whole heart in an undivided way, just as a husband desires that his wife love him with an undivided love. If a wife divides her love among several men, her husband will be envious.

The Ten Commandments tell us that God is a jealous God. Concerning idols, Exodus 20:5 says, "You shall not bow down to them, and you shall not serve them; for I, Jehovah your God, am a jealous God, visiting the iniquity of the fathers upon the children, to the third and fourth generations of those who hate Me." Because God is a jealous God, we should worship only Him and not divide our worship between Him and anyone else. Similarly, 2 Corinthians 11:2 says, "For I am jealous over you with a jealousy of God; for I betrothed you to one husband to present you as a pure virgin to Christ." We should not love the Lord half-heartedly. To love the things of the world even in a small way is to commit spiritual adultery. As His wife, we must love Him with undivided loyalty, with our whole heart. Just as the apostle Paul had a godly jealousy, the indwelling Holy Spirit is jealous over us that we may love God with an undivided love.

Our Human Spirit Being
the Reality and Life of Our Being

James 2:26 speaks of our human spirit. This verse says, "Just as the body without the spirit is dead, so also faith without works is dead." This shows the importance of our human spirit. Without our spirit we are nothing. We are simply dead and empty. We are beings of worth only because we have a human spirit. Therefore, our spirit is the reality of our being, and it is the life of our being. By this brief mention of the Holy Spirit and our human spirit in the book of James, we can realize how much we need to pay attention to the enjoyment of the Holy Spirit in our spirit.

THE SPIRIT OF GLORY AND OF GOD
IN 1 PETER FOR SUFFERING
UNDER THE GOVERNMENT OF GOD

The revelation concerning the Holy Spirit in a book of the New Testament is according to the subject of that book. The four main writers of the New Testament are Matthew, Peter, Paul, and John. The central thought of Matthew's ministry is the kingdom. The main item of Paul's ministry is the church. The main thought of the ministry of John is the fellowship with the Father and with one another in the household, the family, of God. Lastly, the subject of the Epistles of Peter is the divine government. Therefore, the Holy Spirit revealed in 1 and 2 Peter is related to the government of God.

We should not think that God is not governing today.

God truly is governing. If we read 1 Peter carefully, we will see the proper meaning of God's government. Verse 17 of chapter 4 says, "It is time for the judgment to begin from the house of God." God's judgment in His household is a matter of His government. In this book we can see the sufferings of the believers, but we must realize why we need to suffer. The suffering of the believers is a matter of God's government.

The Spirit of Glory and of God
Resting upon Those Who Suffer for the Lord

In our suffering under God's governmental dealing, the Holy Spirit is the Spirit of glory. Verse 14 of chapter 4 says, "If you are reproached in the name of Christ, you are blessed, because the Spirit of glory and of God rests upon you." If we are willing to be persecuted for the Lord and suffer under God's governmental dealing, the Spirit of glory and of God will rest upon us. At the time of his martyrdom, a martyr for the Lord has the Spirit of glory upon him. When Stephen was being tried, those in the Sanhedrin saw his face as though it were the face of an angel (Acts 6:15). This was because the Spirit of glory was resting upon him.

Thirty years ago I met a dear brother, a traveling preacher who had been a businessman, and I asked him how he had been saved. He told me that he was saved as a young man at the time of the Boxer Rebellion in the early 1900s. The Boxers were so prevailing on the streets in Beijing that all the stores were closed for fear of them. One day from within his store he heard a great noise on the street. Looking through the cracks of his door, he saw many Boxers with swords marching and shouting. At the rear of that parade was a mule cart carrying a young Christian girl on her way to be martyred, singing and full of joy. There was a glory on her face. This impressed him very much. He said to himself, "There must be something real about Christianity. How can such a small girl be so bold?" This shocked him. He told himself that he should learn what Christianity is. It was in this way that he was brought to the Lord, gave up his business, and made the decision to serve the Lord with his full time as a preacher.

There is no doubt that the Spirit of glory and of God rested upon that young sister. When we suffer for the name of the Lord, the Spirit becomes the Spirit of glory resting upon us. To be a martyr is not to be put to death with bitterness. Rather, to be a martyr is a matter of gladness and glory. What is suffering to the people of the world is a glory to us, the believers. When we suffer under God's governmental dealing, there is always a glory. The Spirit of glory rests upon us to help us in our suffering, and while we are suffering, this Spirit of glory gives us the hope of glory (Col. 1:27) so that our suffering will be in the way of glory.

The Testifying Spirit Making Clear
the Things of Christ's Suffering and Glory

According to 1 Peter, glory always follows suffering. Verses 10 and 11 of chapter 1 say, "Concerning this salvation the prophets, who prophesied concerning the grace that was to come unto you, sought and searched diligently, searching into what time or what manner of time the Spirit of Christ in them was making clear, testifying beforehand of the sufferings of Christ and the glories after these." The prophecies concerning Christ were made by the Spirit of Christ in the prophets of the Old Testament dispensation. Even before Christ came, His Spirit in the Old Testament was with the prophets who diligently did their best to seek out, to search, and to know what would happen to Christ. At that time the Spirit of Christ signified to them and testified how Christ would suffer and then be glorified. The Psalms and Isaiah in particular have many predictions concerning Christ's suffering and glory (Psa. 22; Isa. 53). The Spirit of glory within us today gives us the understanding that if we suffer with Christ, we will also be glorified with Him.

The Holy Spirit for the Preaching of the Gospel

First Peter 1:12 continues, "To them it was revealed that not to themselves but to you they ministered these things, which have now been announced to you through those who preached the gospel to you by the Holy Spirit sent from heaven, which things angels long to look into." The Holy Spirit in 1 Peter is also the preaching Spirit. It is through Him that the

gospel is preached, and it is through Him that we receive
the gospel to be saved.

The Sanctifying Spirit

Verse 2 says, "Chosen according to the foreknowledge of
God the Father in the sanctification of the Spirit unto the
obedience and sprinkling of the blood of Jesus Christ: Grace
to you and peace be multiplied." In 1 Peter, the Spirit is also
the Spirit of sanctification, the sanctifying Spirit. The gospel
was preached and received through Him. Then after receiving
the gospel and being saved through the Spirit, we are being
sanctified by this same Spirit.

The Spirit with Our Spirit for the Spiritual House and the Spiritual Offerings

Verse 5 of chapter 2 says, "You yourselves also, as living
stones, are being built up as a spiritual house into a holy
priesthood to offer up spiritual sacrifices acceptable to God
through Jesus Christ." To be built up as a spiritual house is to
be built up in the Holy Spirit and in our spirit. Moreover, the
spiritual sacrifices we offer to God are both in the Holy Spirit
and in our spirit. The gospel is preached through the Spirit,
and it is by the Spirit that we received the gospel. Now the
Spirit is doing a work to sanctify us and to build us up as
a spiritual house, a body of priests, to serve God by offering
spiritual sacrifices. Therefore, to be saved, sanctified, built
up, and to serve God are all in the Spirit, who is with us as
the Spirit of glory under God's governmental dealing.

Proclaiming in the Spirit Who Makes Us Alive

Verses 18 and 19 of chapter 3 say, "Christ also has suffered
once for sins, the Righteous on behalf of the unrighteous, that
He might bring you to God, on the one hand being put to
death in the flesh, but on the other, made alive in the Spirit;
in which also He went and proclaimed to the spirits in prison."
Although many Bible scholars find these verses difficult to
understand, the principle here is that genuine preaching is
always carried out by the Spirit who makes alive. Christ was

put to death in the flesh, but He was made alive in the Spirit as the essence of His divinity (Rom. 1:4; cf. John 4:24a), and it is in this Spirit that He went to proclaim the victory achieved by God. In the same principle, when we go out to preach the gospel, we also must proclaim in the Spirit who has made us alive.

The Hidden Man of the Heart, a Meek and Quiet Spirit

First Peter also speaks of our human spirit. Verse 4 of chapter 3 says, "The hidden man of the heart in the incorruptible adornment of a meek and quiet spirit, which is very costly in the sight of God." Because our heart surrounds our human spirit, our spirit is the hidden man of the heart. Such a spirit should be meek and quiet. This is the best adornment before God, especially for the sisters. The sisters should be meek and quiet, not merely outwardly but inwardly in their spirit, that is, in the hidden man within their heart. We usually consider that females are meek and quiet persons. In truth, though, it is difficult to be meek and quiet in the spirit. It is easier to be angry inwardly. The best adornment in the sight of God is a deep meekness and quietness from the innermost, hidden part of the heart. It is not only the sisters who need such a spirit; the brothers also need such a spirit.

Living in the Spirit according to God

Verse 6 of chapter 4 says, "Unto this end the gospel was announced also to those who are now dead, that they might be judged in the flesh according to men but live in the spirit according to God." In order to live according to God, we must live in the spirit. We are made alive in the Spirit, we proclaim in the Spirit, and we live according to God in our regenerated human spirit indwelt by the Spirit of God (John 3:6; Rom. 8:10-11). Everything must be in the Spirit.

THE PROPHESYING SPIRIT IN 2 PETER

Second Peter contains one reference to the Spirit. Verse 21 of chapter 1 says, "No prophecy was ever borne by the will of man, but men spoke from God while being borne by the Holy Spirit." The Holy Spirit bore the prophets, just as wind carries along sailboats. As they were carried along by the Holy Spirit, the prophets spoke from God. Therefore, the Spirit in 2 Peter is the prophesying Spirit.

THE ANOINTING SPIRIT IN 1 JOHN

The Spirit Anointing Us with the Divine Element of God

The subject of 1 John is the fellowship of the children of God with the Father and with one another (1:3, 6-7). This fellowship is first vertical, with the Father, and then it is horizontal, with one another. This is the "family fellowship" in the household of God. In 1 John as a book of fellowship, the Holy Spirit is the anointing Spirit (2:20, 27). Fellowship is possible only by the anointing Spirit. The anointing is not only the ointment itself but also the action of anointing. The indwelling Spirit is constantly moving, working, and acting to anoint us. To anoint is to "paint" with an ointment, to apply the ointment to us. The Holy Spirit within us is always anointing us to put the substance, the divine element, of God into us. The more He anoints us, the more His divine element is "painted" into us. It is by this anointing that we maintain the fellowship between us and the Father and between one another.

The anointing is on the positive side. On the negative side, we also need the cleansing of the blood (1:7). This corresponds with the type in the Old Testament. In type, the blood was first sprinkled on the items of the tabernacle, and then the ointment was applied to the things sprinkled by the blood. In order to have the anointing, we must first have the cleansing of the blood. The sprinkling of the blood paves the way and lays the ground for the anointing. That is why the cleansing of the blood is mentioned in chapter 1, and the anointing of the Spirit is in chapter 2. The cleansing of the blood takes care of the negative things, such as our sins, transgressions, and shortcomings. Then the anointing of the Spirit brings in the positive matter, which is the substance and element of

God. It is by the cleansing plus the anointing that we maintain the fellowship in the household of God. Therefore, the Spirit in 1 John is the anointing Spirit.

The Spirit Being for the Mutual Abiding between Us and God

Verse 24 of chapter 3 tells us that the anointing Spirit is for the mutual abiding between us and God. This verse says, "He who keeps His commandments abides in Him, and He in him. And in this we know that He abides in us, by the Spirit whom He gave to us." Then verse 13 of chapter 4 says, "In this we know that we abide in Him and He in us, that He has given to us of His Spirit." The Lord's abiding in us is by the anointing Spirit.

The Spirit of Truth for Testifying and Discerning

Testing the Spirits to Know the Spirit of Truth

This anointing Spirit is also the Spirit for our discernment. Verses 1 through 3 say, "Beloved, do not believe every spirit, but prove the spirits whether they are of God, because many false prophets have gone out into the world. In this you know the Spirit of God: Every spirit which confesses that Jesus Christ has come in the flesh is of God, and every spirit which does not confess Jesus is not of God; and this is the spirit of the antichrist, of which you have heard that it is coming and now is already in the world." Every spirit that confesses the incarnation of the Lord Jesus, that the Lord Jesus was God incarnated to be a man, is of God. Whoever cannot confess this is not of God. The Spirit of God here is the testifying and discerning Spirit.

Verse 6 continues, "We are of God; he who knows God hears us; he who is not of God does not hear us. From this we know the Spirit of truth and the spirit of deception." The Spirit of truth is the Spirit of God who testifies and confesses that Christ came in the flesh as God incarnate. This is the work of the Spirit which is contrary to the deceitfulness of the false spirits. Many times when a person has a "Pentecostal" experience, he does not feel that it needs to be tested. However, this is against the word of God in 1 John. We need to receive the word that certain manifestations that seem to be of the Spirit should actually be tested.

We saw a particular case like this almost forty years ago in the place where Brother Watchman Nee was. One day while a brother was praying, a voice came to him from the corner of the ceiling, speaking in Chinese. He was very excited, so he called others to come hear that voice speaking. They also became excited and went to Brother Nee. However, Brother Nee read this portion of the Word to them: "Do not believe every spirit." He told them to go back to test the spirit by asking whether or not he would confess that the Lord Jesus came in the flesh as God incarnated to be a man. The next time the voice came, they said to it, "Do you confess that the Lord Jesus came in the flesh, that He was God incarnated as a man?" The answer came back: "Read 1 Corinthians 13." The brothers were very happy since this is a chapter about love. However, Brother Nee said, "He must answer your question yes or no. If he does not answer, he is of the devil" (Matt. 5:37). The brothers went back and told the spirit, "In the name of the Lord Jesus we ask you, do you confess that the Lord Jesus came in the flesh?" At this point the voice said, "Jesus is cursed." Those who were present had an indescribable evil sense. Brother Nee personally told me this story, and many years later another brother who had been there confirmed it. We must not do anything that is not according to the Word. The Word tells us not to believe every spirit but to test them. In particular, we need to test certain so-called manifestations of the Spirit.

The Spirit Testifying That
Jesus Christ Is the Son of God

In 1 John 5 the testimony of God is that Jesus Christ is the Son of God (vv. 1, 9-11). Verses 6 through 8 say, "This is He who came through water and blood, Jesus Christ; not in the water only, but in the water and in the blood; and the Spirit is He who testifies, because the Spirit is the reality. For there are three who testify, the Spirit and the water and the blood, and the three are unto the one thing." Spirit, water, and blood correspond to the major events in the life of the Lord Jesus: His birth, His baptism, His crucifixion, and His resurrection. At the conception of Christ, the Holy Spirit declared that He was the Son of God (Matt. 1:20; Luke 1:35). Then at His baptism, the water bore witness that Christ was the Son of God (John 1:31). When Jesus was baptized, a voice out of heaven proclaimed, "This is My Son, the Beloved" (Matt. 3:16-17). At His crucifixion, the blood also bore witness that Christ was the Son of God (John 19:31-35; Matt. 27:50-54). When Christ was crucified, the centurion declared, "Truly this man was the Son of God" (Mark 15:39). Then in His resurrection, He was designated the Son of God according to the Spirit of holiness (Rom. 1:4). In this principle, the anointing Spirit constantly witnesses that Jesus Christ is the Son of God.

THE SPIRIT FOR OUR PRAYER IN JUDE

Jude 20 says, "You, beloved, building up yourselves upon your most holy faith, praying in the Holy Spirit." The Holy Spirit in Jude is the Spirit for our prayer. We need to pray not in ourselves but in Him. Verse 19 says, "These are those who make divisions, soulish, having no spirit." The people in the world are soulish, not caring for their spirit or using it; they live and walk in the soul. We the believers must use our spirit by praying in the Holy Spirit. However, we may be the same in principle as the worldly people, walking and living in our soul. If this is the case, it will seem that we do not have a spirit. What distinguishes the believers from the unbelievers is that the latter are soulish, not using their spirit, while the former care for their spirit and pray in the Holy Spirit.

We may illustrate the difference between believers and unbelievers in the following ways. When an unbeliever is about to travel, he exercises his mind as to whether he should go by bus or by airplane. This means that he is soulish. However, when a believer is about to travel, he should make his decisions by exercising his spirit to pray. Similarly, the unbelievers exercise their mind and live in the soul to make decisions about their schooling. The believers, though, behave in a different way. Because they have the Holy Spirit within them, they make all their decisions by exercising their spirit to pray in Him. It is regrettable, though, that we sometimes behave the same as the unbelievers do. It seems that we do not have a spirit, that we are soulish. In everything, even in our shopping for example, we need to pray in the Spirit. We should not exercise our mind to buy things in the soul. We need to exercise our spirit to do our shopping with prayer. Unbelievers do not have the Holy Spirit in their spirit, but we the believers do.

Chapter Thirteen

THE SEVEN SPIRITS
FOR GOD'S ADMINISTRATION
IN REVELATION

Scripture Reading: Rev. 1:4-5; 4:5; 5:6; 2:1, 7; 22:17; 19:10; 22:6; 1:10-12; 4:2; 17:3; 21:10

In the previous chapters we saw that in Romans the Spirit is the Spirit of the Son of God for our sonship. In 1 Corinthians He is the building Spirit, and in 2 Corinthians He is the transforming Spirit. In Galatians He is the Spirit for our life and walk, in Ephesians He is the Spirit for the Body, in Philippians He is the Spirit with the bountiful supply, and in Colossians He is the Spirit for our love and wisdom. In 1 and 2 Thessalonians He is the sanctifying Spirit, in 1 and 2 Timothy He is the Spirit for our exercise unto godliness, and in Titus He is the renewing Spirit. In Hebrews He is the eternal Spirit, in James the Spirit of envying, in 1 and 2 Peter the Spirit of glory, in 1 John the anointing Spirit, and in Jude the Spirit for our prayer. Now in Revelation, the Spirit is the seven Spirits of God for God's administration.

Revelation 1:4 and 5 say, "John to the seven churches which are in Asia: Grace to you and peace from Him who is and who was and who is coming, and from the seven Spirits who are before His throne, and from Jesus Christ, the faithful Witness, the Firstborn of the dead, and the Ruler of the kings of the earth." These verses speak of the three of the Triune God. First is Him who is and who was and who is coming, second is the seven Spirits before the throne, and third is Jesus Christ. It is clear from this that the seven Spirits are reckoned as a person in the Triune God.

THE SEVEN SPIRITS AS THE SEVEN EYES OF THE LAMB BEING FOR GOD'S ADMINISTRATION

Chapter 4 speaks of the throne of God as the center of the universe. Verse 5 says, "Out of the throne come forth lightnings and voices and thunders. And there were seven lamps of fire burning before the throne, which are the seven Spirits of God." In the Old Testament, Exodus 25 and Zechariah 4 speak of the lampstand with its seven lamps in type. In the fulfillment of the type in Revelation, the seven lamps are the seven Spirits, who are burning before God for enlightening and judging. Verse 6 of chapter 5 says, "I saw in the midst of the throne and of the four living creatures and in the midst of the elders a Lamb standing as having just been slain, having seven horns and seven eyes, which are the seven Spirits of God sent forth into all the earth." At this point the Lamb is no longer only for redemption. Now He is the Lamb with power, authority, and might, signified by the seven horns. Christ as the Lamb has seven eyes, which are the seven Spirits of God sent forth to fulfill God's purpose throughout the entire earth.

God's Administration
Being Related to His Judgment

As we have seen before, the Holy Spirit is mentioned and applied in each of the Epistles according to the subject of that Epistle. In Romans, for example, He is the Spirit of the Son for our sonship, because Romans shows us how sinners become the sons of God. The book of Revelation unveils the administration of God in His judgment. As the Ruler of the universe, God has His administration, His government. The sixty-six books of the Bible, from Genesis to Revelation, reveal the divine administration in a full way. The first item mentioned in the Bible concerning God's administration is creation. However, after God created all things, this creation became fallen, so the second item of His administration is redemption. The final item in God's administration is judgment. The first two chapters of the Bible are for creation. Then from the third chapter of Genesis to Jude is a long section for redemption under God's mercy and grace and according to His righteousness. God has presented His redemption to man, and we must receive it. If someone does not receive it, the judgment of God will come to him one day. Therefore, in the last book of the Bible there is God's administration in His judgment.

In Revelation there are four great sevens: seven churches (2:1—3:22), seven seals (6:1—8:5), seven trumpets (8:6—11:19), and seven bowls (15:1—16:21). Each of these four "sevens" is a part of God's administration in His judgment. First, the revelation of the seven churches reveals God's administration. Here, the Lord is not mainly the redeeming One but the judging One. The letters to the seven churches in chapters 2 and 3 have much to do with judgment. Likewise, in the vision of the Lord in chapter 1, His appearance is not of the Redeemer but of the Judge. In his Gospel, John could recline on the Lord's bosom (John 13:23), but in Revelation John fell at the Lord's feet when he saw Him (1:17). This is because the atmosphere had changed from redemption to judgment. The Lord Jesus came as the judging One. In chapter 1, His eyes were like a flame of fire (v. 14), but by chapter 4 we see that He has seven eyes. These seven eyes, which are burning lamps, are searching, enlightening, and judging; nothing is hidden from them.

The Spirit as the Seven Eyes of the Lamb Being for the Divine Administration of the Triune God

The seven seals, the seven trumpets, and the seven bowls are also parts of God's administration in His judgment. Therefore, in the book of Revelation the number seven signifies administration in judgment. This gives us the meaning of the seven Spirits. The Spirit of God in Revelation is mentioned as the seven Spirits because here He is not the Spirit of grace but the Spirit for the divine administration through the divine judgment. The Spirit is the seven eyes of the Lamb that can see into things clearly and the seven lamps that are burning and full of light. You can hide certain things from me, and I can hide certain things from you, but none of us can hide anything from the seven eyes of the Lamb. When the Lamb with the seven eyes looks at us, everything is exposed and searched out. Anything that is brought into the light is exposed. These searching and enlightening eyes of the Lord are for judgment. The seven Spirits of God are the burning fire and the searching eyes to search, enlighten, and judge.

In 21:23, the Lamb is the lamp, and God is the light within the lamp. This signifies that God is in the redeeming Lamb. Chapter 5 also tells us that the Spirit is the eyes of the Lamb, which are the shining lamps. God is in the Lamb, and the Lamb has seven eyes. God, the Lamb, and the Spirit as the seven eyes are the three persons of the Triune God. Our eyes are for administration, for directing us. Therefore, in the Triune God, the Father is the source, the Son is the expression, and the Spirit as the seven eyes is the administration. The seven Spirits have been sent into the whole earth for God's administration. We may compare the seven Spirits to the headlights of a car, which are for "administration." Wherever the lights shine, the car drives; the shining of the headlights is for driving, and driving is the administration of the car. Today God is operating in His divine administration, and this administration is through the seven Spirits as the seven lamps and the seven eyes.

THE LORD BEING THE SPIRIT
WHO SPEAKS TO THE SEVEN CHURCHES

Chapters 2 and 3 contain the epistles to the seven churches. Verse 1 of chapter 2 says, "To the messenger of the church in Ephesus write: These things says He who holds the seven stars in His right hand, He who walks in the midst of the seven golden lampstands." No doubt, it is Christ the Lord who is speaking to the church. However, at the end of the epistle verse 7 says, "He who has an ear, let him hear what the Spirit says to the churches." At the beginning of each of the seven epistles, it is the Lord who speaks to a certain church (2:1, 8, 12, 18; 3:1, 7, 14), but at the end of the epistles it is the Spirit who speaks to all the churches (2:7, 11, 17, 29; 3:6, 13, 22). This proves that the Lord is the Spirit (2 Cor. 3:17; 1 Cor. 15:45b) and that He speaks in the Spirit, with the Spirit, and through the Spirit.

It also proves that the Lord is speaking as the Spirit not only to a certain church but to all the churches. The Spirit as the eyes of the Lord looks into the situation of all the churches, and He speaks concerning the whole situation. The Lord as the Spirit speaks to the churches without any limitation of time and space. While the church in a certain locality reads the epistle to Ephesus, the Spirit looks into the church in that locality and speaks to the ones there. The seven Spirits of God are sent forth not only to Ephesus but to Los Angeles, to London, and to the whole earth. The seven epistles in Revelation 2 and 3 are words spoken by the Lord Jesus, but today when we read them, the seven Spirits of God speak these words to us in our spirit for the purpose of God's administration. This proves that the Spirit is one with the Lord, and the Lord is one with the Spirit. The Lord speaks in the Spirit, through the Spirit, and with the Spirit, because He is the Spirit.

THE SPIRIT BECOMING ONE
WITH THE COMPLETED CHURCH AS THE BRIDE

Verse 17 of chapter 22 says, "The Spirit and the bride say, Come!" Chapters 2 and 3 tell us that the Lord speaks with the Spirit, but in this verse the Spirit speaks with the bride. In chapters 2 and 3 the Lord and the Spirit are one, but now at the end of the book the Spirit and the bride are one. When the bride speaks, the Spirit speaks, and when the Spirit speaks, the bride speaks, because these two are one. Perhaps if we were John, we would have said, "The Spirit says, Come! and the bride follows to say, Come!" However, the way John rendered this verse is very meaningful. That the Spirit and the bride say, "Come!" means that the Spirit and the bride have become one.

Moreover, this verse does not say, "The Spirit and the church"; rather, it says, "The Spirit and the bride." This is because the bride is the completed church. There is no doubt that the bride is the church, but the church today may not yet be ready to be the bride. It is when the church truly becomes the bride that it will be one with the Spirit. The church must be completed so that there will be a true oneness between the Spirit and the bride. At that point, the church will be one with the Spirit, who is one with the Lord. In chapters 2 and 3, the Lord speaks in the Spirit and with the Spirit, but in chapter 22 the Spirit speaks in the church and with the church. This Spirit is the seven Spirits of God for God's administration today. He is waiting for the opportunity to permeate the church so that the church may become one with Him as the bride.

TO APPREHEND THE TESTIMONY OF JESUS REQUIRING US TO BE IN THE SPIRIT

The last part of 19:10 says, "The testimony of Jesus is the spirit of the prophecy." The spirit of the prophecy is the reality, substance, disposition, and characteristic of the prophecy, which is the testimony of Jesus for God's administration. If we do not read this book in the spirit, we will receive only the predictions in it concerning the things to come. We will not have any sense, feeling, or realization of Jesus Himself. However, this book of prophecy is not merely a book of predictions about things to come. This book of prophecy is a book full of the testimony of Jesus. Therefore, in reading it we should fully pay our attention to Christ. In order to realize the testimony of Jesus, we need to be in the spirit as John was (1:10; 4:2; 17:3; 21:10). Then as we are in the spirit, this book will attract us to Jesus.

THE LORD BEING THE GOD OF THE SPIRITS OF THE PROPHETS

Verse 6 of chapter 22 says, "He said to me, These words are faithful and true; and the Lord, the God of the spirits of the prophets, has sent His angel to show to His slaves the things which must quickly take place." The Lord is the God of the spirits of the prophets. In the same principle today, the Lord is the God of our spirit and in our spirit. Therefore, in order to contact Him, we need to contact Him in our spirit.

BEING IN SPIRIT TO SEE THE VISIONS IN THE BOOK OF REVELATION

In addition to revealing the four great "sevens," Revelation unveils four great visions: the vision of the churches (chs. 1—3), the vision of the destiny of the world (chs. 4—16), the vision of Babylon the Great (chs. 17—20), and the vision of the New

Jerusalem (chs. 21—22). At the beginning of each of these visions the apostle John says that he was in spirit. Verse 10 of chapter 1 says, "I was in spirit on the Lord's Day and heard behind me a loud voice like a trumpet." In the Greek text, there is no article before *spirit,* indicating that it is our human spirit, which is mingled with God's Spirit. Verse 12 continues, "And I turned to see the voice that spoke with me; and when I turned, I saw seven golden lampstands." John saw the vision of the churches as the seven golden lampstands in his spirit. We need to see all the matters related to the local churches not in our natural mind and understanding but in our spirit. We need to reject our natural mentality and turn to the spirit. There in our spirit we will see the vision of the churches.

Verse 2 of chapter 4 says, "Immediately I was in spirit; and behold, there was a throne set in heaven, and upon the throne there was One sitting." John also saw the vision of the situation of the world in his spirit. Even today, we can understand the real situation of the world only in our spirit. Even the best politicians do not know the true situation of the world. If we are in spirit, the situation of the world will be clear to us.

Verse 3 of chapter 17 says, "He carried me away in spirit into a wilderness; and I saw a woman sitting upon a scarlet beast, full of names of blasphemy, having seven heads and ten horns." This sinful and awful woman is Babylon the Great, the mother of the harlots and the abominations of the earth (v. 5). The scarlet beast is both the Roman Empire and Antichrist, and the woman sitting upon the beast is the apostate Roman Catholic Church. This indicates a confederation between the false religion and worldly politics. Again, the principle is that in order to see the vision of the mysterious Babylon, we need to be in spirit. If we are in spirit, we will be clear that the Roman Catholic Church is the great harlot on the earth (v. 1), the counterfeit of the New Jerusalem that corrupts and damages the Lord's Body.

In the last of the four visions, 21:10 says, "He carried me away in spirit onto a great and high mountain and showed me the holy city, Jerusalem, coming down out of heaven from God." In order to see the vision of Babylon the Great, we need to be in the wilderness, but to see the New Jerusalem we must climb a high mountain in the spirit. We must be in spirit to see the vision of the churches as the seven golden lampstands, the vision of the world situation, the vision of Babylon the Great, and the vision of the New Jerusalem. How much we need to be in spirit! To see the heavenly visions requires us to be in our spirit.

In summary, Revelation tells us that the Spirit of God today is the seven Spirits of God for God's administration in judgment, that the Lord is one with this Spirit in speaking to and dealing with His church, that the Spirit is one with the completed church as the bride, that the Lord is the God of the spirits of the prophets, and that in order to see the heavenly visions we need to be in our spirit. It was in the spirit that the writer of this book, the apostle John, saw the visions concerning all the great matters—the churches, the destiny of the world, Babylon the Great, and the New Jerusalem.

About the Author

Witness Lee was born in 1905 in northern China and raised in a Christian family. At age 19 he was fully captured for Christ and immediately consecrated himself to preach the gospel for the rest of his life. Early in his service, he met Watchman Nee, a renowned preacher, teacher, and writer. Witness Lee labored together with Watchman Nee under his direction. In 1934 Watchman Nee entrusted Witness Lee with the responsibility for his publication operation, called the Shanghai Gospel Bookroom.

Prior to the Communist takeover in 1949, Witness Lee was sent by Watchman Nee and his other co-workers to Taiwan to ensure that the things delivered to them by the Lord would not be lost. Watchman Nee instructed Witness Lee to continue the former's publishing operation abroad as the Taiwan Gospel Bookroom, which has been publicly recognized as the publisher of Watchman Nee's works outside China. Witness Lee's work in Taiwan manifested the Lord's abundant blessing. From a mere 350 believers, newly fled from the mainland, the churches in Taiwan grew to 20,000 in five years.

In 1962 Witness Lee felt led of the Lord to come to the United States, settling in California. During his 35 years of service in the U.S., he ministered in weekly meetings and weekend conferences, delivering several thousand spoken messages. Much of his speaking has since been published as over 400 titles. Many of these have been translated into over fourteen languages. He gave his last public conference in February 1997 at the age of 91.

He leaves behind a prolific presentation of the truth in the Bible. His major work, *Life-study of the Bible,* comprises over 25,000 pages of commentary on every book of the Bible from the perspective of the believers' enjoyment and experience of God's divine life in Christ through the Holy Spirit. Witness Lee was the chief editor of a new translation of the New Testament into Chinese called the Recovery Version and directed the translation of the same into English. The Recovery Version also appears in a number of other languages. He provided an extensive body of footnotes, outlines, and spiritual cross references. A radio broadcast of his messages can be heard on Christian radio stations in the United States. In 1965 Witness Lee founded Living Stream Ministry, a non-profit corporation, located in Anaheim, California, which officially presents his and Watchman Nee's ministry.

Witness Lee's ministry emphasizes the experience of Christ as life and the practical oneness of the believers as the Body of Christ. Stressing the importance of attending to both these matters, he led the churches under his care to grow in Christian life and function. He was unbending in his conviction that God's goal is not narrow sectarianism but the Body of Christ. In time, believers began to meet simply as the church in their localities in response to this conviction. In recent years a number of new churches have been raised up in Russia and in many eastern European countries.

OTHER BOOKS PUBLISHED BY
Living Stream Ministry

Titles by Witness Lee:

Abraham—Called by God	0-7363-0359-6
The Experience of Life	0-87083-417-7
The Knowledge of Life	0-87083-419-3
The Tree of Life	0-87083-300-6
The Economy of God	0-87083-415-0
The Divine Economy	0-87083-268-9
God's New Testament Economy	0-87083-199-2
The World Situation and God's Move	0-87083-092-9
Christ vs. Religion	0-87083-010-4
The All-inclusive Christ	0-87083-020-1
Gospel Outlines	0-87083-039-2
Character	0-87083-322-7
The Secret of Experiencing Christ	0-87083-227-1
The Life and Way for the Practice of the Church Life	0-87083-785-0
The Basic Revelation in the Holy Scriptures	0-87083-105-4
The Crucial Revelation of Life in the Scriptures	0-87083-372-3
The Spirit with Our Spirit	0-87083-798-2
Christ as the Reality	0-87083-047-3
The Central Line of the Divine Revelation	0-87083-960-8
The Full Knowledge of the Word of God	0-87083-289-1
Watchman Nee—A Seer of the Divine Revelation ...	0-87083-625-0

Titles by Watchman Nee:

How to Study the Bible	0-7363-0407-X
God's Overcomers	0-7363-0433-9
The New Covenant	0-7363-0088-0
The Spiritual Man 3 volumes	0-7363-0269-7
Authority and Submission	0-7363-0185-2
The Overcoming Life	1-57593-817-0
The Glorious Church	0-87083-745-1
The Prayer Ministry of the Church	0-87083-860-1
The Breaking of the Outer Man and the Release ...	1-57593-955-X
The Mystery of Christ	1-57593-954-1
The God of Abraham, Isaac, and Jacob	0-87083-932-2
The Song of Songs	0-87083-872-5
The Gospel of God 2 volumes	1-57593-953-3
The Normal Christian Church Life	0-87083-027-9
The Character of the Lord's Worker	1-57593-322-5
The Normal Christian Faith	0-87083-748-6
Watchman Nee's Testimony	0-87083-051-1

Available at
Christian bookstores, or contact Living Stream Ministry
2431 W. La Palma Ave. • Anaheim, CA 92801
1-800-549-5164 • www.livingstream.com